The Adventures of
Arsène Lupin,
Gentleman-Thief

Maurice Leblanc

Level 3
(1600-word)

Adapted by Miki Terasawa

IBC パブリッシング

はじめに

　ラダーシリーズは、「はしご (ladder)」を使って一歩一歩上を目指すように、学習者の実力に合わせ、無理なくステップアップできるよう開発された英文リーダーのシリーズです。
　リーディング力をつけるためには、繰り返したくさん読むこと、いわゆる「多読」がもっとも効果的な学習法であると言われています。多読では、「1. 速く 2. 訳さず英語のまま 3. なるべく辞書を使わず」に読むことが大切です。スピードを計るなど、速く読むよう心がけましょう（たとえば TOEIC® テストの音声スピードはおよそ 1 分間に 150 語です）。そして 1 語ずつ訳すのではなく、英語を英語のまま理解するくせをつけるようにします。こうして読み続けるうちに語感がついてきて、だんだんと英語が理解できるようになるのです。まずは、ラダーシリーズの中からあなたのレベルに合った本を選び、少しずつ英文に慣れ親しんでください。たくさんの本を手にとるうちに、英文書がすらすら読めるようになってくるはずです。

《本シリーズの特徴》
- 中学校レベルから中級者レベルまで5段階に分かれています。自分に合ったレベルからスタートしてください。
- クラシックから現代文学、ノンフィクション、ビジネスと幅広いジャンルを扱っています。あなたの興味に合わせてタイトルを選べます。
- 巻末のワードリストで、いつでもどこでも単語の意味を確認できます。レベル1、2では、文中の全ての単語が、レベル3以上は中学校レベル外の単語が掲載されています。
- カバーにヘッドホンマークのついているタイトルは、オーディオ・サポートがあります。ウェブから購入／ダウンロードし、リスニング教材としても併用できます。

《使用語彙について》
レベル1：中学校で学習する単語約1000語
レベル2：レベル1の単語＋使用頻度の高い単語約300語
レベル3：レベル1の単語＋使用頻度の高い単語約600語
レベル4：レベル1の単語＋使用頻度の高い単語約1000語
レベル5：語彙制限なし

Contents

I. The Arrest of Arsène Lupin *3*

II. Arsène Lupin in Prison *19*

III. The Escape of Arsène Lupin *31*

IV. The Strange Traveler *43*

V. The Queen's Necklace *55*

VI. The Seven of Hearts *69*

VII. Madame Imbert's Safe *95*

VIII. The Black Pearl *103*

IX. Sherlock Holmes Arrives Too Late *117*

Word List *134*

The Adventures of
Arsène Lupin,
Gentleman-Thief

I. The Arrest of Arsène Lupin
ルパン逮捕される

【キーワード】
- [ ] arrest
- [ ] wound
- [ ] evidence
- [ ] innocence
- [ ] conduct
- [ ] disguise
- [ ] crime
- [ ] guilt
- [ ] doubt

【あらすじと登場人物】

　フランスを出発し、ニューヨークに向かうプロバンス号に、「一等船室にアルセーヌ＝ルパンがいる」という無線電信が届くことから、船上では乗客たちがルパン探しにやっきになる。

Detective Ganimard　ガニマール警部　ルパン逮捕に執念を燃やすフランス警察の警部。

Nelly Underdown　ネリー＝アンダダウン　プロバンス号に乗り合わせた美しい令嬢。

Bernard d'Andrézy　ベルナール＝ダンドレジー　プロバンス号に乗り合わせ、ネリーに恋をする。

Marquis de Raverdan　ラベルダン侯爵　プロバンス号の一等船室の乗客。

Rivolta　リボルタ　プロバンス号の一等船室の乗客。髪の黒い、イタリア人。

Rozaine　ロゼーヌ　プロバンス号の一等船室の乗客。ルパンと疑われる。

Lady Jerland　ジャーランド夫人　ネリーの友人で、ニューヨークまでの旅を共にしている。

I.
The Arrest of Arsène Lupin

What a strange journey! Yet it had begun so well.

We were sailing from France to New York. Our ship, *La Provence*, was large and fast. The captain was an excellent man. The passengers were people of culture and style. The pleasure of new friendships made the time pass quickly. We enjoyed being on the ship, away from the world. Our ship was like a little island.

Before our journey, we passengers had been strangers. We had known nothing about each other. But now, on the ship, we felt very close. Our lives seemed to mix. Together we faced the ocean's power. We sailed through wild storms and also calm waters.

In recent years, life at sea has changed. When we are on a ship, we are not truly alone. The outside world can reach us. How, you ask? The answer is the wireless telegraph. This new modern device sends messages through the air. It can even send messages to ships at sea.

On the first day of our journey, many passengers on *La Provence* received telegraph messages. The next day, our ship was 500 miles from the coast of France. The weather was bad. During a terrible storm, the captain received this message:

"Arsène Lupin is on your ship. He is traveling first class. He has light-colored hair and a wound on his right arm. He is traveling alone, under a different name. He is using the name R—"

Suddenly the telegraph stopped. The storm was too strong. The rest of the message was lost. We never learned the name Arsène Lupin was using.

The news spread quickly on the ship. Soon all

I. The Arrest of Arsène Lupin

the passengers knew. We talked of nothing else.

Arsène Lupin was hiding on our ship! Arsène Lupin, the famous gentleman-thief! Lupin stole only from the rich, and he did so with style. Every crime was perfect like a work of art. Even Ganimard, the best detective in France, could not catch him.

Arsène Lupin himself was a mystery. He never looked the same twice. No one really knew who he was—and now he was on *La Provence*!

Everyone on the ship was excited and nervous. "Which one of us is Lupin?" we wondered. "Perhaps this passenger is Lupin! Or maybe that one? Or perhaps he is the man who sits next to me at dinner?"

The next day, a group of passengers discussed Lupin.

"What a situation!" Mademoiselle Nelly Underdown cried. "We have no way of discovering Arsène Lupin. And yet he is on this ship! We must wait until we arrive in New York to find out. I am so nervous. I hope he will be arrested soon."

She looked at me. "Monsieur d'Andrézy, you have spoken with the captain. You must know something about Lupin. Please tell us!" she said.

I wished that I could answer Mademoiselle Nelly. She was a very beautiful young woman. She had a sweet manner. She was a delight. I felt myself in danger of falling in love with her.

Mademoiselle Nelly had grown up in France. Now she was going to America to visit her wealthy father. She was traveling with a friend, Lady Jerland.

"I have no special knowledge, Mademoiselle," I said. "But we can certainly determine who is Arsène Lupin. One does not have to be Detective Ganimard to discover Lupin's secret."

"You have great confidence, Monsieur d'Andrézy," she said with a smile.

"We have all the information we need," I told her.

"What information?" Mademoiselle Nelly asked.

"First, we know that Lupin calls himself Monsieur R—. Second, he is traveling alone. Third, he has light-colored hair. Now let's look at the list of first-class passengers."

I had the list in my pocket. I took it out and read it. Then I said, "On this passenger list, there

1. The Arrest of Arsène Lupin

are only thirteen men whose names begin with *R*. Nine of them are traveling with other people. Only four men are traveling alone. Of these four, one must be Lupin."

"Who are these four men?" Mademoiselle Nelly asked.

"First is the Marquis de Raverdan," I told her.

"He is not Lupin! That would be impossible. I have known the Marquis for years," she said.

"Next is Major Rawson," I continued.

"He is my uncle," someone else said. "Major Rawson is definitely not Lupin."

"Third is Monsieur Rivolta," I said.

"I am Monsieur Rivolta," an Italian gentleman answered. He had very black hair.

"He is not Lupin," Mademoiselle Nelly smiled. "His hair is not light-colored!"

"Then the answer is simple," I said. "The fourth man must be Arsène Lupin."

"Who? Who is he? What is his name?" Mademoiselle Nelly asked.

"Monsieur Rozaine," I told her. "Does anyone know him?"

For a moment, no one answered. Then Mademoiselle Nelly turned to a quiet, thin young man. "Monsieur Rozaine, what do you say?" she asked.

All of us looked at the young man. His hair was light-colored. "Yes, I am traveling alone," he said. "My hair is light, as you can see. According to the evidence, I must be Lupin. Perhaps I should be arrested now."

Monsieur Rozaine was making a joke, of course. It seemed impossible that this young man could be the famous Lupin. And yet...Rozaine's voice seemed to shake. He seemed nervous.

"Do you have the wound?" Mademoiselle Nelly asked Rozaine. "Lupin has a wound on his arm. That is what the telegraph message said."

"No," Rozaine said. "I do not have the wound." He showed us his arm.

I was not fooled, however. Rozaine had showed us his left arm. Lupin's wound was supposed to be on his right arm.

Suddenly Lady Jerland ran to us. "Help!" she cried. "My jewels! Someone has stolen my jewels! They were taken from my room!"

The crime was quite strange. The thief had not taken all the jewels. He had taken only the best and most beautiful stones. He had left the others.

I. The Arrest of Arsène Lupin

All the passengers had the same thought. Arsène Lupin has stolen the jewels!

That night, the captain arrested Monsieur Rozaine. Everyone on the ship felt better. Rozaine *was* Lupin, after all. The gentleman-thief had been caught. We were safe again! The ship was secure!

But in the morning, the captain freed Monsieur Rozaine. He had been able to prove his innocence. Neither of his arms had a wound like Lupin's. Also, Rozaine was far away from Lady Jerland's room when the jewels were taken. Finally, he had papers that proved who he was. Monsieur Rozaine was not Arsène Lupin.

Then Monsieur Rozaine announced that he would give 10,000 francs to anyone who could catch Arsène Lupin. "If no one can catch that criminal, then I will find him myself," Rozaine said.

For several days, Rozaine searched the ship. The captain of *La Provence* also conducted a search. Every room was examined. But neither Rozaine nor the captain could find Lady Jerland's jewels. They did not find Arsène Lupin, either.

Everyone on the ship became more and more

nervous. Who was Lupin? Where had he hidden the jewels?

On the third afternoon, I walked around the ship with Mademoiselle Nelly. She and I had spent every day of the journey together. I loved her beauty and sweet nature. As we walked, I took photographs with my camera.

"Lupin may be a master thief," Mademoiselle Nelly said. "But we know that the jewels are hidden somewhere, Monsieur d'Andrézy! They are somewhere on the ship."

"That is true," I agreed. "The captain should search everyone's bags. He should examine any objects that belong to us."

Then I held up my camera. I showed it to Mademoiselle Nelly. "For example, Lupin could use a camera to hide the jewels. He could put the jewels inside and then pretend to take photographs. No one would guess his secret."

That night Monsieur Rozaine could not be found. The captain ordered a search of the entire ship. Finally, one of the ship's officers found the poor Monsieur Rozaine. He was not hurt, but his money had been stolen. Then he had been tied up with rope and left in a dark corner of the ship.

1. The Arrest of Arsène Lupin

He never saw the thief who had attacked him.

But the thief had left a message in Rozaine's pocket. The note said: "Arsène Lupin thanks Monsieur Rozaine. Lupin is very happy to accept his 10,000 francs."

All the passengers were very afraid now. Lupin had struck again! None of us wanted to be alone. For safety, we stayed in groups. But danger seemed to surround us. Nobody trusted anyone else. Each and every passenger was a suspect now. Any person among us could be Lupin!

After all, this gentleman-thief was a master of disguise. He could change his face, change his voice, and change his name so easily! *Who was Arsène Lupin?* Everyone on the ship had a different theory. No one could agree. All we could do was wait until the journey ended, until we reached New York.

During this time, Mademoiselle Nelly stayed by my side. I was glad to protect her, to make her feel safe. I felt strangely grateful to Arsène Lupin... He was bringing Mademoiselle Nelly and me closer together. I was in love with her, I realized. I suspected that she loved me, too.

There were no new messages from the

telegraph. It was silent. The lack of news was terrible. We lived in fear. Our thoughts became wild. We expected the worst...that another crime would occur. This time, we thought, it would be worse than a theft. It would be death! It would be murder! Lupin was in control, we felt. He was the true captain of the ship. Our money and our lives were his, if he wanted them.

At last *La Provence* arrived in New York. Our journey was over. Finally we would find out who was Arsène Lupin! Everyone prepared to leave the ship. There was great excitement among the passengers.

Then the moment arrived. I will never forget it. Mademoiselle Nelly and I stood on the ship. We looked at the crowd of people waiting below. The police were there, too.

I pointed to the police. "Look, Mademoiselle Nelly," I said. "The police are here. They are probably waiting for Arsène Lupin."

"Will they catch him?" she asked. Her voice was strangely worried.

"Who knows?" I said. "Maybe Lupin has already escaped. Or perhaps he preferred to die rather than be arrested. He may have jumped

I. The Arrest of Arsène Lupin

into the ocean."

"Oh, do not say such a thing!" Mademoiselle Nelly cried.

Then I saw another man in the crowd. He was an older man. His face was very ordinary. He wore a plain green coat.

I pointed at him. "Do you see that man in the green coat?" I asked Mademoiselle Nelly. "That is Ganimard."

"Ganimard, the famous detective?" she said.

"Yes. He is the enemy of Arsène Lupin. He is here to arrest him," I told her. "Now I understand why we received no more telegraph messages during our journey. That was because of Ganimard. He always keeps his business secret."

The passengers started to leave the ship. The Marquis de Raverdan left. So did Major Rawson and Monsieur Rivolta. But Ganimard did not seem interested in them.

"Perhaps Monsieur Rozaine is Lupin," said Mademoiselle Nelly. "Ganimard will certainly arrest him!"

Rozaine started to leave the ship. He was about to pass Ganimard. I handed my camera to Mademoiselle Nelly.

"You should take Rozaine's photograph," I said. "It would be interesting to have a picture with both Rozaine and Ganimard in it."

But Ganimard paid no attention to Rozaine. So, Rozaine was not Arsène Lupin!

"Who is Lupin?" Mademoiselle Nelly cried. "If Rozaine is not Lupin, then who is?" She looked around the ship. Only twenty passengers were left. "One of them must be Lupin," she said.

"It is time to leave the ship," I said. "We cannot wait much longer."

We started to leave. Mademoiselle Nelly was still holding my camera. Then Detective Ganimard stepped in front of us.

"What is it?" I asked him.

"One moment, monsieur," he said. "What is your name?"

"I am Bernard d'Andrézy," I said.

"Impossible!" Ganimard answered. "Bernard d'Andrézy died three years ago. You are Arsène Lupin."

"You are wrong," I said. "Everyone knows that Lupin is traveling under the name R—"

"That is another trick," Ganimard said. "You

1. The Arrest of Arsène Lupin

created the story of that name yourself. You were trying to fool people."

Then Ganimard hit my right arm. I cried out in pain. He had hit the wound described in the telegraph message.

I had to give myself up. It would be impossible to escape. With a smile, I allowed Ganimard to arrest me.

I looked at Mademoiselle Nelly. She had heard every word. She looked back at me. Then her beautiful eyes looked down at my camera.

I knew that she suddenly understood everything. The jewels of Lady Jerland were hidden inside my camera. Monsieur Rozaine's 10,000 francs were also hidden there. In her hands, Mademoiselle Nelly held all the evidence of my crimes! If she told Ganimard, he could prove my guilt.

But what would Mademoiselle Nelly do? Would she tell Ganimard? Would she give him the camera?

Her face was perfectly calm. I could not tell what she was thinking. Did she hate me now? Or was it possible that she still cared for me? I dared not say a word.

Then Mademoiselle Nelly turned away. She did not say goodbye. She was leaving the ship with the other passengers.

Suddenly Mademoiselle Nelly dropped the camera. She had done it on purpose, I knew. The camera fell over the side of the ship and into the water. It sank into the sea. It was gone forever!

No one saw what Mademoiselle Nelly had done. The jewels and the money were gone! Now there was no evidence against me!

For a moment, I stood silently. Then I said, "What a pity that I am not an honest man!"

* * * *

That was the story of Arsène Lupin's arrest. He told me the story himself. He has told me about his other adventures, too. I am honored to record these adventures in writing.

What does Arsène Lupin look like? I have been asked that question many times. But I cannot describe him. Each time I see him, he looks completely different. He is a master of disguise. He can change his face and voice so easily.

"Why should I let anyone recognize my face?"

1. The Arrest of Arsène Lupin

he said to me. "My actions speak loudly enough. When the public sees my work, they know it is mine! No one else has done what I have. When people see my actions, they say with no doubt: 'Arsène Lupin did that!'"

II. Arsène Lupin in Prison
獄中のアルセーヌ＝ルパン

【キーワード】
- [ ] treasure
- [ ] warn
- [ ] horn
- [ ] drug
- [ ] clue
- [ ] cell
- [ ] admit
- [ ] so-called
- [ ] trial

【あらすじと登場人物】
　堅牢な城、マラキ城の城主に、獄中のルパンから手紙が届く。ルーベンスの絵、宝石、家具などをいただくというのだ。

Baron Nathan Cahorn　ナタン＝カオルン男爵　マラキ城の主。有名絵画、宝石などを収集する金持ち。

Monsieur Dudouis　デュドウイ警察部長　本事件を担当する。

Detective Ganimard　ガニマール警部　ルパンを逮捕して休暇をとっている。

II.
Arsène Lupin in Prison

Many stories are told about the castle of the Malaquis. This old castle is built on a rock. It sits in the middle of the Seine.

For years, the castle belonged to the Baron Nathan Cahorn. The Baron was a very rich man. He owned many treasures: paintings by Rubens and Watteau, beautiful jewels, fine furniture.

The Baron loved his treasures more than anything. His greatest fear was losing them. He kept the castle carefully guarded. No one was allowed inside. High walls and strong gates protected it.

One day the Baron received a strange letter. He

opened it and read:

Monsieur le Baron:

You own a very fine large painting by Rubens. You also have a lovely small painting by Watteau. I also like your jewels and your Louis XIII table.

For now, these few objects are enough for me. Please send them to the Batignolles train station. I will pick them up at the station. I will expect to receive them by next week.

If you do not send these objects to me, I will visit your castle and take them myself. I will come on the night of September 27th.

Arsène Lupin
Prison de la Santé, Paris

P.S. Please do not send your large painting by Watteau. Although you paid a lot of money for it, it is not the real painting. It is just a copy.

The Baron was confused and in shock. The letter was from the famous Arsène Lupin, gentleman-thief. But that seemed impossible! Lupin was now

II. Arsène Lupin in Prison

in prison in Paris. Ganimard had arrested him in America and brought him back to France. How could Lupin steal the Baron's treasures when he was in prison?

But the Baron was still worried. He asked the police for their help. But the police laughed. "Lupin is in prison," they said. "He cannot steal your treasures, Monsieur le Baron."

Then the Baron read a story in the local newspaper. The story said that Ganimard was on vacation in the city. He had come to rest after catching Arsène Lupin. The Baron hurried to find the famous detective.

The Baron soon found Ganimard. He told the detective about the strange letter. "Will you help me?" he asked.

Ganimard laughed. "You do not need my help," he said to the Baron. "A real thief would never warn you before stealing your treasures. The letter must be a joke. Anyway, the letter cannot be from Arsène Lupin. He is in prison. He cannot escape. He certainly cannot steal from you! Go home, Monsieur le Baron. Your treasures are safe."

The Baron felt better. Perhaps Ganimard was

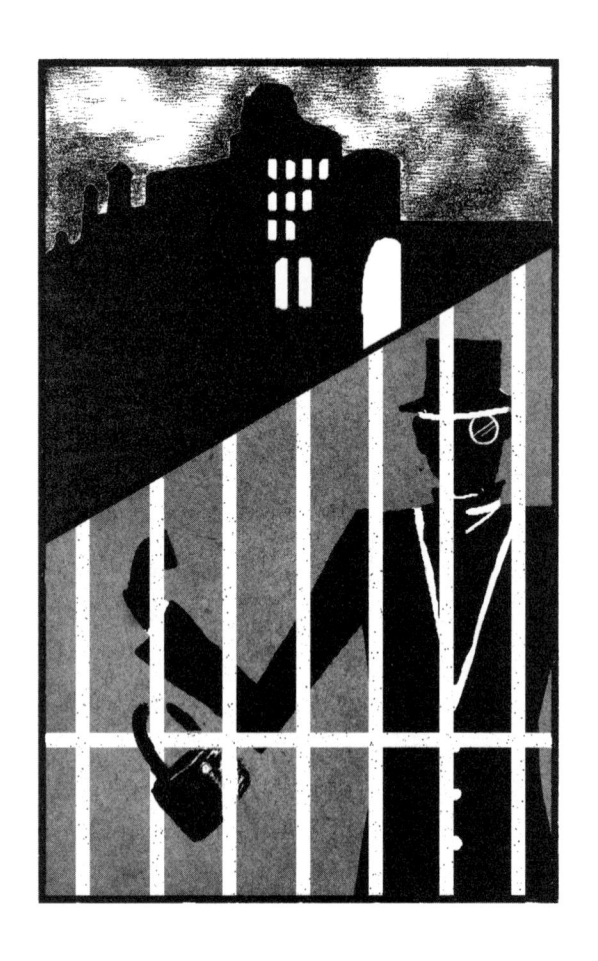

II. Arsène Lupin in Prison

right. The letter must be a strange joke. Lupin was in prison, after all. There was no danger.

Six days passed. It was September 26th. Then the Baron received another letter. It read:

You have not sent the objects to me. Therefore I will come to the castle tomorrow night and take them. — Arsène

The Baron was very afraid now. He hurried back to Ganimard. "You must help me, Ganimard!" he cried. "Please come to my castle tomorrow. You must stop Lupin! I will pay you to help me."

"I am on vacation," Ganimard said. "As a police detective, I am not supposed to accept other work. It would be wrong."

"No one will know," said the Baron. "I will keep it secret. And I will pay you 3,000 francs."

Finally the detective agreed. "I will come to your castle tomorrow. I will bring two of my men with me."

On the night of the 27th, Ganimard arrived with his two men. They carefully searched the castle. They studied the room where the treasures were kept.

"There is no way Lupin can get in. The castle is guarded well," Ganimard told the Baron. "The doors and windows are locked. But my men will watch and wait. If Lupin does come, they will be ready."

Ganimard's two men stayed in the room with the treasures. Ganimard and the Baron stayed nearby. The night passed quietly. At midnight, they heard the horn of a car. "Do not worry," Ganimard said. "It is just a car driving by."

In the morning, Ganimard and the Baron went to see the treasures. They entered the room. To their shock, Ganimard's two men were asleep. All the treasures were gone!

"My paintings! My jewels! My table!" the Baron cried. "How did Lupin get in?"

Ganimard was even more shocked. "My men!" he cried. "They have been drugged. This is the work of Arsène Lupin!"

"What should I do?" the Baron cried.

"Call the police," Ganimard said. "Tell them it was Lupin. But don't mention my name! I will try to help you, but it must be a secret."

"If Arsène Lupin will return my treasures, I will do anything!" the Baron said. "I will even

II. Arsène Lupin in Prison

pay him."

Ganimard looked up. "Then perhaps the situation is not without hope. Would you be willing to pay Lupin 100,000 francs?" he asked.

"Yes, yes!" the Baron said. "I will gladly pay 100,000 francs if Lupin will give back my treasures."

Ganimard and his men left the castle. Then the Baron called the local police. They searched everywhere, but they found no clues. It seemed impossible. How did Lupin steal the Baron's treasures? The castle had high walls and strong gates. The doors and windows had been locked. No one could have gotten inside! It was a mystery.

The local police had no answers. They asked the Paris police for help. The captain of the Paris police was Monsieur Dudouis. He called Detective Ganimard. Together they discussed the situation.

"Searching the castle is a waste of time," Ganimard said. "I must speak with Arsène Lupin. He knows the truth."

"Lupin!" said Dudouis. "But he is in prison. It's impossible that he stole the treasures."

"Lupin is the only man in France who could

have planned this crime. Nothing is impossible for him. I must speak with him," Ganimard answered.

Finally Captain Dudouis agreed. Ganimard went to visit Lupin in prison.

The detective entered Lupin's cell. "My dear Ganimard!" Lupin cried. "It is a pleasure to see you."

"You are very kind," Ganimard said.

"I wish I could offer you a drink," Lupin said. "But this cell is not designed for receiving guests. Please forgive me. I will only be here for a short time, you know."

The detective smiled. "For a short time?" he said. "Really?"

Lupin smiled back. "So why are you here, my dear Ganimard?" he asked.

"I wanted to ask you about Baron Cahorn's treasures," the detective answered.

"Ah! The castle of the Malaquis," Lupin said. "Yes, I was happy to accept the Baron's treasures."

"So it was you!" Ganimard said. "The letters? You sent them?"

"Yes, I sent him both letters."

"But what was the purpose? You were having fun with the Baron, I imagine."

"No," Lupin said. "You must think, Ganimard! The castle is well guarded, you know. It is too difficult to break in. There is only one way to get inside… The Baron himself had to invite me inside. The letter was the first step."

"That is an original idea," Ganimard admitted. "But how exactly?"

"I told the newspaper that a famous detective was in the area. The newspaper reported the story, which the Baron read. Then the Baron hurried to ask for the famous detective's help. But in reality, this 'detective' was a friend of mine… another thief! The Baron invited this so-called detective into the castle. The rest was easy. Once inside, it was simple to steal the treasures."

"A very good plan!" Ganimard said. "But you must have used the name of a real detective. Who was it? It had to be someone famous to get the Baron's attention."

"I used your name, my dear Ganimard."

The detective looked shocked.

Lupin laughed. "It is perfect, isn't it? Ganimard against Ganimard! You really should arrest yourself now."

Ganimard did not laugh. To him, the joke was not funny.

"Do not look so angry," Lupin told him. "Baron Cahorn will get his treasures back. My friend, the so-called Ganimard, has fixed it. The Baron will pay me 100,000 francs. Then I will return his treasures to him."

Ganimard stood up. "Thank you for explaining this to me," he said. "But Lupin, you really should be thinking about your trial. You are still in prison, you know."

"For now," Lupin said. "I have decided not to attend my trial."

Now Ganimard was laughing. "Oh really?" he said. "You have no choice, Lupin. You will attend your trial."

"My dear Ganimard, you do not understand. I, Arsène Lupin, stay here in prison of my own free will. I will leave when I want to. You cannot stop me."

"Then why did you let me arrest you?" Ganimard asked.

Lupin smiled. "When you arrested me, I was thinking about something far more important. I was thinking about a woman whom I loved. At that moment, nothing else mattered."

"Lupin, you are quite romantic," Ganimard said. "But I don't think you can escape from prison. I still expect to see you at your trial."

"I will be sorry to disappoint you," Lupin answered. "But we will certainly see each other again. Just not at my trial."

The two men shook hands and said goodbye. Ganimard left the cell. He locked the door carefully behind him.

III. The Escape of Arsène Lupin
　　ルパンの脱獄

【キーワード】
☐ courthouse　　☐ bow　　　　　☐ prisoner
☐ refuse　　　　☐ address　　　☐ beggar
☐ reason　　　　☐ innocent　　 ☐ appearance

【あらすじと登場人物】
　ラ・サンテ刑務所にいるルパンが脱獄を計画していることを察知した警察は、逆に泳がせて仲間も一網打尽にしようとするが……。

Captain Dudouis　デュドゥイ警察部長　ガニマール警部の上司。

Désiré Baudru　デジレ＝ボードリュ　ルパンの身代わりに牢やに入れられていた浮浪者

III.
The Escape of Arsène Lupin

Arsène Lupin was sitting in his cell in the Prison de la Santé. He was speaking with Captain Dudouis of the Paris Police.

"I will not attend my trial," Lupin said. "My dear sir, there is nothing you can do. I will not be at my trial." He smiled politely.

"We will see about that!" the captain said. He hurried out of Lupin's cell.

"Watch Lupin carefully," Dudouis told his police officers. "He must not escape! Guard him well. Search his cell! He may be hiding something!"

One day, Lupin was brought to another part of the prison. While he was there, the police searched his cell. They found a fine cigar. Hidden inside the cigar was a note. It read:

The plan is ready. The time has come. When you are inside, press your foot down. The floor will open. Then you will be free. We will find you.

Captain Dudouis read the note. He was very pleased. "Aha!" he said. "I was right! Lupin is planning to escape soon. This is what we will do. We will allow him to escape, but we will be watching the entire time. We will find out where Lupin lives. Then we will catch him again and put him back in prison. If we are lucky, we will also catch his helpers."

The captain carefully put the note back inside the cigar. He put the cigar back in Lupin's cell. "He must not know that we read this note," Dudouis said. "Lupin must suspect nothing."

Several days later, the police took Lupin to the courthouse. A judge was going to question him. "Monsieur Lupin," the judge said. "I will ask

III. The Escape of Arsène Lupin

you questions today. You must tell us about your crimes. Answer carefully. These questions will be important during your trial."

"I will be happy to tell you about my crimes," Lupin said. "But it may take a long time. There are so many of them!" he laughed. "But these questions are not important at all."

"Why not?" asked the judge.

"I will not be at my trial," Lupin told him. The judge was angry, but there was nothing he could do.

Then it was time to leave the courthouse. The police had to take Lupin back to the Prison de la Santé. They put him in a special police car. Inside the car was a cell where Lupin sat. The car began to drive back to the prison.

As the car reached the Bridge Saint Michel, something happened. Inside the car, Arsène Lupin pressed his foot down on the floor of his cell. There was a clicking sound. Then suddenly the floor slid away, and a hole appeared. In one quick movement, Lupin slipped through the hole. He was free!

The car drove away. The police did not seem to notice that Lupin had escaped.

Lupin walked along the bridge. He did not run or hide. He walked for a while, enjoying the day. The weather was bright and sunny. Then Lupin stopped at a café. He sat and drank a cup of coffee. Then he went to the owner of the café. In a loud voice he said, "I don't have any money right now. However, I will gladly pay you for the coffee in a few days."

"But who are you, monsieur?" the café owner asked. "How do I know that you will pay?"

Lupin bowed. "I am Arsène Lupin," he said. "I am a prisoner at the Prison de la Santé. Right now I am just taking a little walk."

The café owner was shocked. The other people at the café laughed loudly. Then Lupin smiled and walked away slowly. He headed back towards the prison.

Lupin knocked on the prison gates. He politely announced himself to the guards. "It is I, Arsène Lupin," he said. "I have had a pleasant walk. Now I wish to return to my cell in the prison. But first, please call Police Captain Dudouis. I must speak with him."

When Captain Dudouis appeared, he tried to look angry. In reality, he was very surprised that

III. The Escape of Arsène Lupin

Lupin had returned to the prison.

Lupin said, "Don't play games with me, Captain. I know what you tried to do. You let me escape today. As I walked through Paris, your police officers were following me. You wanted to find out my secrets! But you cannot fool Arsène Lupin. When I really do escape, you will not be able to stop me." Then Lupin returned to his cell.

Now Dudouis was truly angry. "Lupin must not escape!" he said. "Move him to a different cell. He must be closely guarded."

In his new cell, Lupin did very little. Most of the time, he lay on the bed and faced the wall. He said almost nothing. He refused to see any visitors. He caused no trouble for the guards.

Every day Captain Dudouis asked the guards, "Has Lupin escaped yet?"

"No, captain," the guards answered.

"Probably he will try tomorrow," Dudouis answered.

After two months, the date of Lupin's trial arrived. All of Paris was interested. Everyone wanted to see the famous Arsène Lupin, gentleman-thief. Everyone thought that the prisoner would try to escape during the trial.

A large crowd of people attended the first day of the trial. They were excited to see Lupin. But when he appeared at the courthouse, Lupin seemed different. He was very thin. He walked slowly, like an old man. His face was gray and tired. His eyes were dark and empty. His mouth hung open.

The crowd was very disappointed. Could this be the famous Arsène Lupin? This man had no energy, no style, no elegance. What was wrong with Lupin? Was he sick? Had he given up? Had prison life defeated him?

Detective Ganimard was in the courthouse, too. He looked at the prisoner once. Then he looked at him again closely. Then Ganimard jumped up in shock. He ran to speak to the judge.

"Excuse me," Ganimard said. "That man... that man is not Arsène Lupin!"

"What do you mean?" the judge asked in surprise. "It must be Lupin!"

"No," said Ganimard. "This man has a similar face, yes. But look carefully. You will see that he is not Lupin! I know Lupin... That is not him."

Captain Dudouis looked at the prisoner, too.

III. THE ESCAPE OF ARSÈNE LUPIN

He studied his face carefully. "Ganimard is right," he said finally. "This man is not Lupin. He looks a bit like Lupin, but his face and body are different in many ways."

The judge addressed the prisoner. "Prisoner, what is your name?"

The prisoner looked up at the judge slowly. He did not seem to understand.

The judge repeated his question. "What is your name?"

The prisoner answered slowly. "My name... my name is Désiré Baudru," he said. His voice was rough and tired. He sounded nothing like Arsène Lupin.

Everyone in the courthouse cried out in surprise and wonder. "He is not Lupin!" "Impossible!" "Lupin has escaped, I knew it!" "How did he do it?"

"Silence!" cried the judge. The crowd became quiet. "Then where is Lupin?" the judge asked Baudru. "Where is he? You must have helped him escape!"

Baudru looked very confused. "Arsène who?" he asked.

After many questions, the story slowly became

clear. Désiré Baudru was a beggar. He lived on the streets of Paris. Two months ago—on the same day Arsène Lupin had escaped from the police car—Baudru had been arrested. He had been put in a cell at the Prison de la Santé. He did not know why, he said. He had done nothing wrong.

"I didn't mind being in prison," Baudru told the judge. "It was warm. I had a bed. I got lots to eat."

The prison guards had no answers, either. "We were told that this man was Arsène Lupin," the guards said. "He was very quiet. He stayed in his cell. Most of the time, he lay on his bed and faced the wall. He never caused trouble. We had no reason to suspect him."

Captain Dudouis was very angry. Somehow Lupin had escaped! He and Baudru had changed places, it seemed. Captain Dudouis wanted to keep Baudru in prison, but he could not. No one could prove that Baudru was working with Arsène Lupin. He seemed to be an innocent man.

"We must let Baudru go free," Detective Ganimard said to Dudouis. "But I will follow him after he leaves the prison. Somehow he is part of Arsène Lupin's plan. I am sure of it. If I follow

III. The Escape of Arsène Lupin

Baudru, he will lead me to Lupin."

"Very well," said Dudouis. "We will release Baudru right away."

Désiré Baudru was released that afternoon. He walked slowly out of the prison. He seemed confused and lost. He appeared to have no idea where he was going.

Ganimard followed Baudru all afternoon. After a while, the detective started to have doubts. "Perhaps this old beggar is really innocent," he said to himself. "Perhaps he has nothing to do with Lupin. Am I wasting my time?"

At last, Baudru came to a large park. The park was green and quiet. There were no other people around. Baudru lay down under some trees. He fell asleep in the sun. He snored loudly in his sleep.

Ganimard looked at the beggar sleeping. "What am I doing?" the detective thought. He was angry with himself. "There is no reason to follow this man. I will return to the prison."

Ganimard turned to leave the park. Suddenly he heard laughter. He turned around quickly.

Baudru was awake now. He was sitting up and laughing.

That laugh! Ganimard knew it well. He was filled with a terrible feeling of surprise.

"Lupin! Arsène Lupin!" Ganimard cried.

"Yes, my dear Ganimard, it is I," Lupin answered. He was still laughing. Suddenly he looked very different. He no longer looked like an old man. He was young, active, full of energy and life again. He was Lupin!

"But…but how? You…Baudru? It was always you?"

"Yes, it was always me. Baudru never existed," Lupin said.

"How…how did you do it?" Ganimard cried.

"It was very simple," Lupin said. "I can change the way I look very easily. It just takes time. One does a few exercises of the face and body. Repeat them hundreds of times, and one's appearance becomes very different."

"But how did you fool the guards?" Ganimard asked.

"I had two months in prison to change my looks. I changed them so slowly that the guards did not notice it," Lupin told him.

"I was so sure," said Ganimard. "In the courthouse, at your trial, I was certain that you were

III. THE ESCAPE OF ARSÈNE LUPIN

someone else! I was certain you had escaped!"

"That was the most important thing," Lupin said. "You believed that I would escape. Everyone believed that I would escape! Once that belief was created, the rest was easy. You wanted to believe that I was Baudru—so you did believe it! It was a simple trick of the mind." Lupin laughed again. "But now, my dear Ganimard, I must say goodbye. We will see each other again soon, I'm sure."

Ganimard was silent. There was no way to arrest Lupin now. The park was quiet, and the two men were alone. The police were far away.

"What will you do next?" he asked Lupin.

"I will enjoy myself. Life in prison was not very fun. But now I must hurry home! I am going to a dinner party tonight, you see."

"A dinner party?" Ganimard asked. "What? Where?"

"Society demands my time," Lupin said with a smile. "Tonight I dine with the British ambassador!"

IV. The Strange Traveler
ふしぎな旅行者

【キーワード】

- [ ] servant
- [ ] conductor
- [ ] blow
- [ ] rob
- [ ] wallet
- [ ] untie
- [ ] description
- [ ] footprint
- [ ] gunshot

【あらすじと登場人物】

ルーアン行きの列車の中で、ルパンは暴漢に襲われる。金品を奪われ縛られたルパンを乗せた列車が駅につくと、そこには警察が来ていた。

Guillaume Berlat ギョーム＝ベルラ 友人のいるルーアンに向かう。

Officer Delivet ドリベ刑事 ルパンを追跡する。

Officer Massol マッソル刑事 ルパンを追跡する。

Pierre Onfrey ピエール＝オンフレー 殺人事件の犯人。列車で強盗を働き逃走。

Madame Renaud ルノー夫人 列車の乗客。

IV.
The Strange Traveler

This story begins with a train journey. I was about to travel by train from Paris to Rouen. From Rouen, I planned to drive my car to visit some friends. These friends knew me only as Monsieur Guillaume Berlat. They did not know my true name: Arsène Lupin!

The day before my train journey, I ordered my servant drive my car to Rouen. There it would wait for me.

The next day, I boarded the train in Paris. I entered my cabin and sat down. The only other passenger in the cabin was a lady. At first, she seemed afraid of me. Then I lifted my hat and bowed to her. That seemed to make her feel better. She smiled politely.

Suddenly a man opened the cabin door and rushed inside. His appearance was a surprise. The lady cried out in fear. She held her bag in her hands.

Certainly, this man's sudden appearance was a shock. But I did not understand why the lady was so afraid. The man was well dressed. He looked like a gentleman. Then I studied his face. "I have seen this man before," I said to myself. "But where? I do not remember."

I looked back at the lady. Her face was white with fear. "Do you...do you know who is on this train?" she said very quietly to me.

"Who?"

"That man...that man... He is Arsène Lupin!" she said.

"Impossible!" I said. "How do you know he is Lupin?"

"He must be," she answered. "The police spoke to the train conductor. Lupin was seen at the Paris station today. The police are planning to search the train when it arrives at Rouen."

IV. The Strange Traveler

"How exciting!" I said with a smile. "But if Arsène Lupin is on this train, he will certainly find a way to escape before we reach Rouen."

"But everyone on the train is in danger!" the lady said.

"My dear madame, I promise you that there is no danger from Arsène Lupin," I told her. I knew that I was right. "If you will excuse me, I will get some sleep."

I quickly fell asleep. But I did not sleep for long. A sharp blow hit my face, and I awoke. The other man had hit me, and his hands were around my neck! I was in shock. I could not move. I could hardly breathe.

On the other side of the cabin, the lady watched helplessly. She dared not scream. Her eyes were filled with fear.

The man took the lady's bag. He also took my wallet, with all my papers. Then, using a rope, he tied me up. He was skilled; his movements were quick and easy. He was definitely a professional criminal.

There I lay, helpless on the floor. What a strange situation! I, the great Arsène Lupin, was being robbed. In a way, the situation was almost funny. And yet, the situation was also very serious. The police were going to search the train at Rouen—and here I was, tied up and unable to escape.

What could I do? There were two problems to solve. First, I had to get my wallet and papers back from the thief. The wallet itself was not important. But the papers were very important. All of my plans and ideas were in them.

Second, I had to make the police believe that I was not Arsène Lupin. Would they believe that I was Monsieur Guillaume Berlat? My escape depended on that.

For now, the thief sat calmly in the cabin. He opened the lady's bag and took out the jewels inside. He opened my wallet and counted the money. Luckily he did not pay attention to my papers.

Then the train slowed down. The thief stood up. He looked out the window. It was raining, but I could see that we were in the countryside near Rouen. Quickly the thief took my gray coat and the lady's umbrella. He opened the cabin door and jumped out of the train. He landed safely and ran away.

IV. THE STRANGE TRAVELER

"What will we do!" the lady cried. "Lupin is gone! He took my jewels and your wallet, monsieur!"

"Do not worry, madame," I told her. "As soon as we reach Rouen, you must call for help. The police will be at the station, you know."

"Let me untie you, monsieur," she said.

"No," I told her. "The police will want to see everything the thief did. You must leave me tied up for now."

"What should I tell the police?" she asked me.

"You must give your name and my name, too. I am Monsieur Guillaume Berlat. If necessary, tell the police that I am a friend of yours. There is no time to lose… We must keep their attention on Lupin! And you must describe Lupin to the police, madame. He took your umbrella, remember? He wore a gray coat—"

"That coat was yours, wasn't it?" she asked.

"No," I told her. "It was not mine. The coat belonged to him. Do you remember now?"

"Oh, yes," she said. "I think that I remember now…"

The train arrived at the Rouen station. The lady began to call for help. "Arsène Lupin…

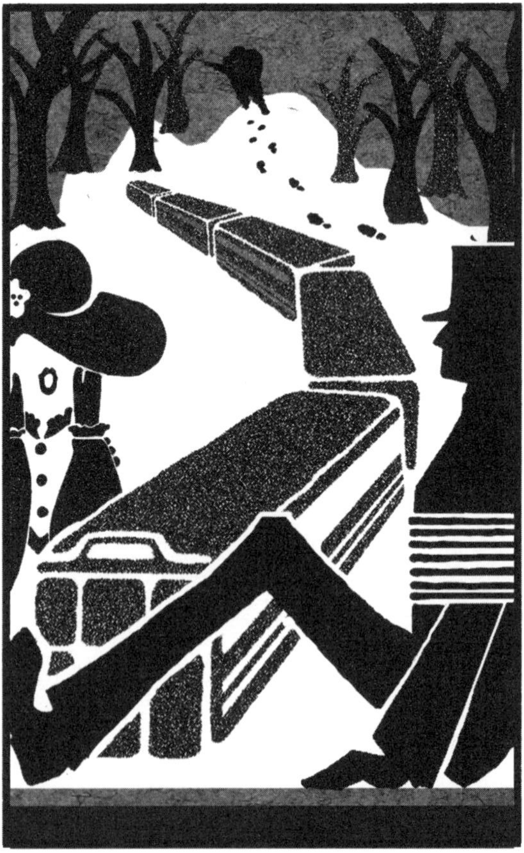

IV. THE STRANGE TRAVELER

He attacked us and then escaped! Lupin stole my jewels... I am Madame Renaud. This is my friend Monsieur Berlat... Lupin tied him up!"

The Rouen police rushed into our cabin. They untied me and began to ask questions. "What did Lupin look like, Madame Renaud?" the police captain asked.

"He had a gray coat," she told the captain. "And he took my umbrella!"

"A gray coat? That sounds right," the captain said. "That matches the description from Paris."

"Captain, we are losing time!" I said. "Every moment that passes, Arsène Lupin is escaping."

"Be patient, Monsieur Berlat," the captain told me. "We must question you and Madame Renaud first. My officers will try to catch Lupin. It will be very hard, though, I fear. Lupin is a master thief."

I had to get away from the police, I knew. It was dangerous to spend so much time with them. It was possible they might recognize me. Also, I wanted to catch the real thief. He still had my papers!

I looked at the captain. "Perhaps I can help, captain. I think I know where Lupin is hiding," I said.

"You, monsieur?" the captain said. He looked very surprised. "You know where he is hiding? How is that possible?"

Had I said too much? I did not want the captain to suspect me. Did he realize that I was the real Lupin?

"I watched him carefully on the train," I said. "I saw the place where he escaped. And I want to get my money back! Quick! We have no time to lose!"

"Oh, yes," cried Madame Renaud. "Perhaps we can get my jewels back, too. Please listen to Monsieur Berlat, captain!"

Thank heavens for Madame Renaud! Her words had the effect I desired. The police captain listened to her. He no longer seemed to suspect me.

"My car is here at the Rouen station," I told the captain. "It is very fast. We can easily find Lupin."

"Very good!" the captain said. "I will send two of my officers with you, Monsieur Berlat. Here is Officer Delivet and Officer Massol."

Moments later, I was driving in my car with

IV. The Strange Traveler

Delivet and Massol. What a strange situation! Arsène Lupin was off to catch Arsène Lupin... with the help of the police! We drove into the countryside near Rouen.

"Here is the place!" I cried. I stopped the car. The two police officers got out. "This is where Lupin jumped out of the train. I saw him running into the trees. We can follow him on foot now."

Delivet, Massol, and I headed towards the trees. My plan was working well so far. But what would I do next? Somehow I had to get my papers back—without the police officers seeing them! That would not be easy.

Then I saw footprints on the ground. The thief had been here! I turned to Delivet and Massol. "Officers, I have a plan. Delivet, you stay to the right. Massol, stay to the left. Guard these areas. I will go and find Lupin. Then I will chase him towards you. Together you can surprise him, catch him, and arrest him. If I need your help, I will fire two gunshots."

Delivet and Massol agreed. They stood in their places while I headed into the trees. The thief was near! I followed his footprints easily. Soon I found him. He was hiding behind a tree.

I hit the man on the head. He fell to the ground, his eyes closed. Then I reached into his pocket. Inside, I was happy to find my wallet and papers. I also found Madame Renaud's jewels.

Then I looked at the man's face again. Suddenly I recognized him. He was Pierre Onfrey, the murderer! He had recently killed a woman and her two daughters in Paris. It had been a terrible crime. Onfrey's face had appeared in all the newspapers. That was why I had recognized him.

"Delivet and Massol will be glad to arrest him," I said to myself. "Arsène Lupin is glad to help the police arrest this murderer." Quickly I wrote a short note to the officers. I signed it with my real name. With the note I left Madame Renaud's jewels and also two hundred francs as a gift to the officers. I put the note next to Onfrey, who still lay silent on the ground.

"Now it is time for me to go," I said with a smile. I picked up Onfrey's gun, fired two shots into the air, and escaped!

The next day, this story appeared in the newspaper *L'Echo de France*:

Yesterday afternoon, the gentleman-thief

IV. The Strange Traveler

Arsène Lupin arrested the murderer Pierre Onfrey. Earlier that day, the murderer had robbed passengers on the train from Paris to Rouen. He had taken a lady's jewels, a wallet, and some papers. Arsène Lupin caught Onfrey and got the stolen objects back. Lupin also gave a generous gift to the police officers who helped him catch Onfrey.

V. The Queen's Necklace
女王の首飾り

【キーワード】

- [ ] courtyard
- [ ] honestly
- [ ] unkind
- [ ] unsigned
- [ ] fail
- [ ] claim
- [ ] transom
- [ ] blame
- [ ] accuse

【あらすじと登場人物】

　マリー・アントワネットゆかりの「女王の首飾り」が、盗まれた。密室の中で誰が盗んだのか、結局解明できないままに十数年が過ぎた。

Madame Du Barry　デュ・バリー夫人　ルイ15世の愛人。

Marie-Antoinette　マリー・アントワネット

Dreux-Soubise　ドルー＝スービーズ伯爵　「女王の首飾り」を先祖代々、家宝として守っている。

Monsieur Valorbe　バロルブ氏　警察署長。

Henriette　アンリエット　スービーズ伯爵夫人の友人で、家政婦として雇われている。

Raoul　ラウール　アンリエットの6歳になる息子。

Rouzières　ルジェール伯爵　スービーズ伯爵の古くからの友人。

Chevalier Floriani　フロリアーニ勲爵士　スービーズ伯爵とイタリアで知り合い、館に招かれた。

V.
The Queen's Necklace

The "Queen's necklace" is famous in French history. This priceless necklace of gold and jewels was made for Madame Du Barry. At one time, it belonged to Marie-Antoinette, Queen of France! More recently, the necklace belonged to the noble Count and Countess de Dreux-Soubise. It had belonged to their family for almost one hundred years.

The Dreux-Soubise were very proud of the Queen's necklace. The Countess only wore it to very special events. The rest of the time, the necklace was kept in the bank.

One night, the Countess de Dreux-Soubise wore the Queen's necklace to a ball. She and the Count returned home very late. The Countess undressed and took off the necklace. She gave it to her husband.

It was too late to take the necklace to the bank, so the Count hid it in their bedroom. He had no fear of thieves. The room was safe. There was only one door, and it had a strong lock. The only window faced an inner courtyard of the house. The window was also closed. A small chest covered the bottom part.

The Count locked the bedroom door. Then he and Countess went to sleep. In the morning, the Count got up first. He planned to take the Queen's necklace back to the bank.

But when the Count looked for the necklace, he could not find it. He and the Countess searched everywhere for it. They found nothing. The famous Queen's necklace was gone!

Finally, the Count called the police. Monsieur Valorbe, the police captain, came quickly to the house. Valorbe searched the bedroom, too. He looked at the door and the window. Then he turned to the Countess.

V. The Queen's Necklace

"Did any of your servants know that you were wearing the necklace last night?" he asked.

"Of course," she said. "I did not hide the fact. But nobody knew where the necklace was hidden in our bedroom."

"No one knew?" Valorbe repeated.

"No one...unless—" the Countess stopped. "Perhaps...Henriette? Her room is across from ours. Her window faces ours."

"Who is Henriette?" Valorbe asked.

"Henriette and I went to school together," the Countess explained. "She fell in love and married a man who was not noble. Her family was very angry. They refused to see her. They threw her out of the house. Henriette had no money. She and her little son had nowhere to go, so we invited them to live here. Henriette does some work for me."

"We will go and speak with her now," Valorbe said.

Henriette's room was small and cold. When Valorbe and the Count and Countess entered the room, they found Henriette sitting with her son Raoul. He was just six years old.

Valorbe looked at Henriette. She was still

young, but her face was marked with great sadness. Little Raoul looked up at his mother lovingly.

When Henriette was told about the crime, she was shocked. "The Queen's necklace is gone!" she cried. "But how?"

Monsieur Valorbe asked Henriette many questions. She seemed to answer honestly. "Last night, I helped the Countess get ready for the ball. I helped her put on the necklace myself. But I did not steal it, monsieur!"

Afterwards, the Count spoke with Monsieur Valorbe. "You cannot suspect Henriette," he said. "She is an honest woman. Anyway, it seems impossible! The window was closed and locked. Our door was locked. I don't know how the thief could have gotten in…and I can't imagine how he escaped."

Valorbe had to agree. After months of searching, the police could find nothing. The mystery of the lost necklace could not be solved.

The Count and Countess were very angry. Losing the Queen's necklace hurt their pride. The Countess still suspected Henriette. She had never been kind to her. Now she began to treat

V. The Queen's Necklace

Henriette badly. Finally, the Countess threw Henriette and her son out of the house.

Several months later, the Countess received a strange letter. It was from Henriette. It read:

Madame, I must thank you. You are so kind to me and Raoul. It was you, was it not? No one else knows where I live. Thank you, thank you for your gift…

What did the letter mean? The Countess was confused. She had done nothing for Henriette. In fact, she had been very unkind. She wrote to Henriette and asked her to explain.

Henriette wrote back. She told the Countess that she had received a letter recently. Inside the letter were one thousand francs. The letter was unsigned. There was no name or address for the sender. Henriette did not know who had sent it.

Over several years, Henriette received more strange letters with money. She never knew who had sent them. It was a mystery! But the money was enough to support Henriette and her son.

Henriette died a few years later. She never discovered the source of the money.

Twenty-five years passed. Only today is the truth known. It happened like this.

One week ago, the Count and Countess de Dreux-Soubise held a dinner party. Among the guests were the Count's cousins, the Marquis de Rouzières, and the Chevalier Floriani. The Marquis was the Count's oldest friend. The Chevalier Floriani was a newer friend. He had recently traveled to Paris from Italy.

After dinner, one guest happened to mention famous crimes. Then the Marquis de Rouzières asked about the Queen's necklace. "Has the theft of the necklace ever been explained?"

"No," said the Count. "Many years have passed, but the necklace was never found. The crime was never explained."

"How did the crime happen?" the Chevalier asked. "I have heard of the Queen's necklace, of course. But I do not know the story of its theft."

The Count told the story. The Chevalier Floriani and the other guests listened carefully. Then the Chevalier spoke.

"I am not a detective," he said calmly. "But the truth is easy to see here. I know how the necklace was stolen."

V. The Queen's Necklace

"Impossible!" cried the Countess. "The police tried to solve the crime for months. They failed. How can you claim to know the truth?"

"We must look at the facts," the Chevalier answered. "The bedroom door was locked from the inside. It was impossible to enter through the door. Therefore the thief entered through the window. That was the only way."

"But how?" the Count asked. "How did the thief cross the courtyard? He could not have jumped from Henriette's window to ours. It is too far! He would have fallen."

"The thief probably made a simple bridge," the Chevalier said. "He used a long piece of wood that reached over the courtyard."

"Where would the thief get such a long piece of wood?" the Countess asked. "Someone would have noticed him carrying it. They would have suspected him."

"Anyway, the window was locked!" the Count said. "We checked it. The police checked it, too! No one had opened the window all night."

"Tell me, does the window have a transom?" the Chevalier asked. The Count and Countess looked confused.

"Is there a transom — a smaller window above the main part?" he asked again.

"Yes, I believe so," the Count said slowly.

"If you check the transom," said the Chevalier, "I think you will discover something strange. I think you will discover that the transom has been opened."

"I will go upstairs and look," the Count told him. "Our bedroom is unchanged. Everything is the same as on the night of the crime."

The Count left his guests. He rushed upstairs to the bedroom. He returned very quickly. His face was white with surprise. "Yes, there is a transom," he cried. "It is not locked...and it has been opened!"

The Count and Countess looked at the Chevalier. "It seems that you are correct, Chevalier," the Countess said. "There is a transom. But you forget something. The transom is extremely small. No man could fit through it! It would be impossible!"

Everyone looked at the Chevalier. He smiled. "Yes, it would be impossible for a man," he said. "But it would not be impossible for a child."

"A child!" the Count cried. "Henriette had a

V. The Queen's Necklace

child. She had a son, Raoul!"

"It must have been Raoul," the Chevalier said. "He was the thief. It all makes sense. No one would suspect a child. Tell me, are there long wooden shelves in Henriette's room?"

"Yes," said the Countess. "But why do you ask?"

"Those shelves are long pieces of wood," the Chevalier explained. "This little boy Raoul... He must have used one of those pieces of wood to make a bridge. That was how he crossed over the courtyard. He placed a long piece of wood between his window and yours. Then he walked across. He opened the transom and climbed through. He entered your room and took the

Queen's Necklace. Then he escaped back through the transom. It was so simple."

The Countess was angry. "It must have been Henriette's idea! She must have planned it. Then she made her son steal the necklace! Terrible woman! She was a criminal!"

"Do not blame Henriette. She had nothing to do with it," the Chevalier said. "She knew nothing." He looked at the Countess. "Henriette wrote to you, didn't she? After you threw her out of this house, she wrote and thanked you. If she had been the thief, she would not have done that. Clearly, she was innocent. The thief was her son."

The Countess was silent. All of the guests looked at the Chevalier Floriani. A strange feeling filled the room.

The Count tried to laugh. "You should become a detective, Chevalier," he said. "That was a very interesting story. You have thought of everything!"

"One has only to imagine the mother and son's lives," the Chevalier said with a sad smile. "Henriette was poor and sick. She had been badly treated for years. She had been thrown out of

V. The Queen's Necklace

your house. The young boy loved his mother. He worried about her. He sold the jewels from the necklace. He sent the money to his mother. The money made her last years easier. The mother died. Many years pass. The boy becomes a man. And now...perhaps the man returns to the house where his mother was a servant...Perhaps he meets the people who treated his mother so badly...the people who accused her of being a thief...Imagine the feelings of such a meeting!"

The Count and Countess were in shock. Clearly, the Chevalier Floriani was Henriette's son! He seemed to admit it now! He had come back to the scene of the crime. He seemed proud of it!

"Who...who are you?" the Count asked.

"I? I am the Chevalier Floriani," the other said. "We have met several times, my dear Count."

"Then what is this strange story?" the Countess demanded.

"Oh, it is just a story!" the Chevalier said. "I simply imagine the pleasure that Henriette's son would have in explaining his crime to you. It would be a great pleasure for him."

The Count did not know what to do. Should

he call the police? But what would he say? The Chevalier Floriani was the thief of the Queen's necklace. He had admitted it! But there was no proof. The police would never arrest him.

The Count decided to pretend that he did not understand. He laughed. "My dear Chevalier, thank you for telling us this story. I enjoyed it very much," he said. "I do have a question, though. What happened to this young man? Today, does he still lead a life of crime? To steal the Queen's necklace at the age of six! That is an excellent way to begin. What do you think happened to Raoul?"

"Stealing the Queen's necklace was an excellent beginning!" the Chevalier agreed. "Raoul is probably a master criminal now…a master thief." Then he turned to the Countess. "My dear Countess, I must say goodbye now. Thank you for listening to my little story."

"Wait, please," said the Countess. "I have a question, too. Do you think that the Queen's necklace still exists, Chevalier? The jewels may be gone now, but does the necklace itself still exist?"

"I imagine that the necklace does still exist," the Chevalier said. "It is a part of French history,

V. The Queen's Necklace

after all. I do not think that Raoul would destroy it."

The Countess paused for a moment. "If you should ever meet this man, Chevalier, would you tell him this? Please tell him that the necklace still belongs to the family of the Dreux-Soubise. Even without the jewels, the Queen's necklace is our pride and joy."

"I will tell him," the Chevalier Floriani answered with a smile. Then he bowed to the Count and Countess and left. The Chevalier was never seen again.

Four days later, the Countess entered her bedroom. She noticed a strange box on a table. She opened the box. Inside, she found the Queen's necklace.

The next day, a story appeared in the *Echo de France*. It read:

> *Arsène Lupin has found the famous Queen's necklace, which was stolen many years ago. Lupin has returned the necklace to the Count and Countess of Dreux-Soubise. What a kind and noble action by the great gentleman-thief!*

VI. The Seven of Hearts
ハートの7

【キーワード】

- [ ] warfare
- [ ] threaten
- [ ] blackmail
- [ ] scared
- [ ] reveal
- [ ] faint
- [ ] revenge
- [ ] fake
- [ ] proper

【あらすじと登場人物】

「わたし」の家に何者かが侵入し、トランプの「ハートの7」のカードを1枚残していった。盗んでいったものはないようだ。そこから事件は国家を巻き込む潜水艦開発の秘密にまで及ぶ。

Jean Daspry ジャン＝ダスプリ 私の友人。

Captain Dudouis デュドウイ警察部長 マイヨー通りの自殺事件を追う。

Georges Andermatt ジョルジュ＝アンデルマット パリに妻と住む大金持ち。実業家。

Etienne Varin エティエンヌ＝バラン バラン兄弟の弟。「わたし」の家で自殺する。

Alfred Varin アルフレッド＝バラン バラン兄弟の兄。弟といくつもの犯罪に手を染める。

Salvator サルバトール エコー・ド・フランス紙の記者。

Louis Lacombe ルイ＝ラコンブ 自殺現場の家に十数年間住んでいた技術者。

Madame Andermatt アンデルマット夫人 ラコンブとは愛人関係だった。

VI.
The Seven of Hearts

People often ask me, "How did you meet Arsène Lupin? Why does he trust you? Why did he choose you to record his adventures?"

The truth is that Lupin did not choose me. He came into my life by chance, as you will soon learn. This is the story of how I first met Arsène Lupin.

This story begins on the night of June 22. That evening, I ate dinner with my friend Jean Daspry. Then I walked home. At the time, I was living at 102 Boulevard Maillot.

When I reached the house, it was dark and empty. As I entered, I suddenly felt afraid. Something felt wrong. Was I being watched? "There is no reason for fear," I told myself. Still, the feeling did not go away. I decided to place my gun next to my bed.

In my bedroom, I saw something strange. There was a letter on my bed. It was addressed to me. I did not recognize the writing. I opened the letter and read it. This is what was written:

From this moment, you are in terrible danger tonight. Whatever happens, whatever you hear, do not move! Do not speak! Stay silent and still! Do nothing, or else you will die!

I was filled with the greatest fear. I dropped the letter. I fell onto the bed. I closed my eyes and did not move.

Then I heard a terrible noise! It sounded like a loud crash. The noise came from the library room, which was next to my bedroom.

"There are thieves in the house," I said to myself. "They are in the library. They are stealing everything! But what can I do? Nothing!" The

VI. THE SEVEN OF HEARTS

noises continued all night. I listened, too afraid to fall asleep.

The noises stopped early in the morning. The house was finally quiet. Carefully I stood up. I picked up my gun and walked to the library door. "They have probably stolen everything," I thought. Then I opened the door.

What I saw filled me with surprise. Nothing had been stolen! Everything was in its place! I saw all my books and art, all my business papers, all my money. "What happened last night? Was it just a bad dream?" I wondered. "Did I imagine all those noises?"

Then I realized that it was not a dream. I looked down at the floor. There I saw a small, bright piece of paper. I looked closely. It was an ordinary playing card: the seven of hearts.

But there was something strange about the card. Each heart had a small hole in it. The holes were perfectly round, as if they had been cut with a knife.

I spent the rest of the day in the library. I searched the room from top to bottom. The thieves had been here... They had dropped the playing card...but what had they been looking for? I wanted to find out.

The library was a strange room. The walls were painted with pictures of kings and gods. The pictures were beautiful, but I did not like them much. I had bought the house just one year ago. I knew nothing about the last owner.

I searched all day but discovered nothing else. "What should I do next?" I wondered. There was no reason to call the police; nothing had been stolen. But the events of the night were so strange!

At that time, I was working as a newspaper reporter. I decided to write about my experience. The next day, my article appeared in the newspaper.

That same afternoon, a man came to my door. He did not look like a gentleman. In fact, he looked like a man who knew much about crime. I almost shut the door in his face. Before I could, however, he spoke to me.

"Wait, monsieur," he said. "I read your article in the newspaper. I must talk to you about it. Is everything you said true?"

"Yes," I told him. "But what is your name?"

"My name is not important," he said. "But

VI. The Seven of Hearts

perhaps I can explain your strange experience. Will you let me? First, though, I must do something."

"What?" I asked.

"I must be alone in your library for three minutes. Will you allow that?" he asked.

"That is a strange request," I said. "But all right! You may be alone in the library for three minutes. I will wait outside the door."

The man went into the library and shut the door. I waited outside. One minute passed, then two minutes... At exactly three minutes, I heard a terrible sound. It was a gun shot!

I rushed into the library. The man lay dead on the floor. He had shot himself in the head. A gun was by his side.

Then I saw something else. Another playing card lay on the floor. "It is the seven of hearts again!" I cried. Like the other card, this one also had seven little holes in it.

I hurried to call the police. Captain Dudouis arrived quickly with his officers. They searched the library. But they could find nothing. The police had only questions, no answers. Why had this man come to my house? Who was he? What had he been looking for in the library? Why had he killed himself?

"He must have been looking for something," I said to Dudouis. "When he could not find it, he killed himself. That is the only idea I have."

"But why?" the captain said. "This is a mystery."

Then an officer looked in the dead man's pockets. He found a small piece of paper. These words were written on it: *Georges Andermatt, 37 Rue de Berry*.

Monsieur Andermatt was famous. He was a rich man of business. He lived here in Paris with his beautiful wife. Why did the dead man have his name?

Captain Dudouis called for Monsieur Andermatt. "Please ask him to come here now," he said. "Tell him to come to 102 Boulevard Maillot."

Monsieur Andermatt arrived at the house quickly. The police explained the situation to him. They showed him the body of the dead man.

"Do you know this man?" Captain Dudouis asked.

Monsieur Andermatt did not want to speak at

VI. The Seven of Hearts

first. Finally he said, "Yes. I knew this man. His name was Etienne Varin. But I have only seen him once before. I did business with his brother, Alfred Varin. That was many years ago, though."

"Why do you think Varin had your name?" Dudouis asked.

"I don't know," Monsieur Andermatt said. "It must be chance. Many people know my name. But I have nothing to do with him!"

Captain Dudouis thanked Monsieur Andermatt and let him go. "There is nothing more we can do here," the captain told me. "It is a very strange situation, but there is no crime here."

I did not believe Monsieur Andermatt's story, though. I described everything that had happened to my friend Jean Daspry. He was very interested, too. Like me, Jean did not believe Andermatt's story.

"Andermatt is keeping something secret. I wonder what it is," he said.

Then the mystery seemed to grow. Jean Daspry and I read an interesting article in the newspaper:

The German navy is testing a new kind of submarine ship. This new ship is very powerful. It will change naval warfare forever. The Germans are trying to keep it a secret. Only two details are known. This new submarine is called the "Seven of Hearts." A French scientist created the submarine's design.

"The Seven of Hearts!" Jean Daspry cried. "Perhaps your little mystery is part of something much bigger, my friend."

I laughed. "You are imagining too much," I told him.

But I was quickly proved wrong. The next day, another article appeared in the *Echo de France*. It was signed "Salvator."

Ten years ago, there was a young French scientist named Louis Lacombe. He came to Paris to work. He lived at 102 Boulevard Maillot.

Lacombe wanted to build a new kind of submarine. He worked for many years. At last, he finished his design for the submarine. He called it the "Seven of Hearts."

Lacombe met two businessmen, the brothers Etienne and Alfred Varin. The

VI. The Seven of Hearts

Varins introduced Lacombe to the rich banker Georges Andermatt. Monsieur Andermatt was interested in the submarine, too. He wanted to help Lacombe sell the design to the French navy. The navy would then build the Seven of Hearts.

The deal was almost done. Louis Lacombe was ready to give the submarine design to Andermatt and the French navy. But one night, Lacombe disappeared. He was never seen again. The design for the submarine also disappeared.

I have discovered that the Varin brothers have the submarine design. They stole it from Louis Lacombe. The Varins have sold the design to the German navy. This action was a crime. It was a crime against Louis Lacombe. It was also a crime against France!

The German navy recently tested the new submarine. I am glad to report that their tests did not succeed. The submarine does not work. This is because the Germans are missing one thing: a final piece of paper written by Louis Lacombe before he disappeared. On this paper, Lacombe wrote some very important, very secret details about his design. Without these details, the Seven of Hearts will never work correctly.

Where is this paper? Only one man can help me find it. That man is Georges Andermatt. Until now, Monsieur Andermatt's actions have been strange. After Louis Lacombe disappeared, he did not call the police. He has kept everything secret.

I, Salvator, now ask Monsieur Andermatt to help me. Alfred Varin is looking for this paper, too. We must find it before he does. We must do this for France!

Everyone in Paris was talking about this article. Where was Louis Lacombe? Why had he disappeared? Who had the paper with the secret details? Did Georges Andermatt have it? And who was the strange Salvator, the author of the article?

The next day, my friend Jean Daspry came to my house. He and I sat in the library. We discussed the article. Suddenly we heard noises in the hall. Then a woman entered the room. She wore a hat that covered her face.

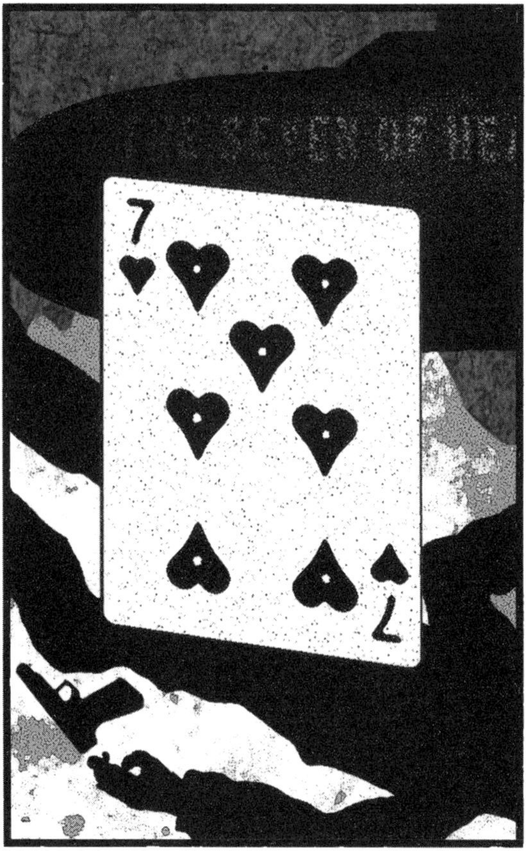

"Monsieur, I must speak with you," she told me. "I must talk to you about the Seven of Hearts."

"Who are you, madame?" I asked.

She slowly took off her hat. Her face was beautiful, but her eyes were sad. "I am Madame Andermatt," she said.

"Madame Andermatt!" I cried. I was very surprised.

Jean Daspry did not seem surprised. "Madame Andermatt," he said. "May I ask you some questions?"

"Yes," she answered.

"Did you know Louis Lacombe?" Daspry asked.

"Yes, he was a friend of my husband," she said.

"Was he also *your* friend?" Daspry asked.

Madame Andermatt stopped for a second. Her face was red. "Yes, he was my friend," she said softly. "In fact, Louis Lacombe was more than just a friend. He and I were lovers."

"Did you ever write to him?" Daspry asked.

"Yes, I wrote many letters to him," Madame Andermatt said. "That is why I am here. Alfred

VI. The Seven of Hearts

Varin has my letters to Louis Lacombe. Varin stole them. He is threatening to publish them."

"Does your husband know about the letters?" Daspry asked.

"Yes, he knows about them," Madame Andermatt said. "Varin told him. But my husband has not read the letters himself."

"So Alfred Varin is blackmailing you and your husband!" I cried.

"Yes," she said. "That is why my husband did not call the police right away. He did not want the police to know about my letters." She began to cry. "I love my husband. I am sorry for what I did! If only I had my letters back... I would destroy them. Then I could start a new life with my husband. If the letters were gone, then I'm sure he would love me again. But I have no hope!"

"There is hope, Madame Andermatt," Daspry said. "Salvator will get those letters from Alfred Varin. He is your friend. He will also get the design for the submarine."

"Salvator?" Madame Andermatt asked. "The man who wrote the article in the newspaper?"

"Yes," said Daspry. "On the night of June 22, Salvator came to this house. In the library, he discovered Louis Lacombe's secret hiding places. Salvator knows where the letters and the submarine design can be found. I am sure of that!"

"Salvator seems to know so much!" Madame Andermatt said. "Will he help me? Will he destroy the love letters? I must trust him. There is no one else I can trust. What must I do?"

"Just answer one more question," Daspry said. "Does your husband have the piece of paper from Louis Lacombe—the one with the secret details about the Seven of Hearts?"

"Yes, he has it," she said. "The night before Louis disappeared, he gave that paper to my husband."

"Very good!" Daspry cried. "That is excellent news. Now, please go home, Madame Andermatt. Trust Salvator... He will help you."

Madame Andermatt left the house. She seemed calmer and less sad.

After Madame Andermatt left, I turned to Daspry. "You have great confidence in this Salvator!" I laughed. "But Salvator has not explained everything yet. Remember those playing cards? The seven of hearts? I found one card on the floor after the night of June 22. I found the

VI. The Seven of Hearts

second card next to the body of Etienne Varin. What about those cards? What is the meaning of the seven of hearts?"

Daspry smiled at me. "Wait and see, my friend! Wait and see! I am sure that Salvator will explain everything."

"What should we do now?" I asked.

"Let's look for Louis Lacombe's hiding places in this house," Daspry suggested. "If we work hard, we may find them."

Daspry and I searched the house. We found nothing. Then we searched in the garden.

"Something is hidden here," Daspry said. "I will dig in the ground."

For several hours, he dug in the garden. It was hard work. He made a deep hole in the ground. Then he cried out. He had found something terrible: human bones!

I was shocked. "Someone was killed and buried here!" I cried. "Who can it be?"

Daspry's face was dark. "Can you not guess?" he said. "These bones belonged to Louis Lacombe. He was murdered. Look!"

I looked up. Daspry was holding a small piece of metal in his hand. The metal was in the shape of a playing card. There was a design of seven red hearts on the metal, with seven small holes cut into them.

"It is the seven of hearts again!" I cried. "What does it mean?"

"It is the key to this strange story," Daspry answered. "Somehow, the seven of hearts opens up Louis Lacombe's secret hiding place. That hiding place is in the library. I am sure of that!"

For the next two days, Daspry searched the library from top to bottom. I did not help him. I felt sick and scared. The discovery of the bones had filled me with fear. I stayed in bed and let Daspry search.

On the third day, I received a strange letter. It read:

My dear sir:

On the night of June 22, I visited your house. You were very kind and did not stop me. For that, I thank you.

Now I must ask you for another favor. Once again I must visit your house. I will arrive tonight at 9. Several "guests" will also arrive. Do not be afraid…it is all part of my

VI. The Seven of Hearts

plan.

The affair of the Seven of Hearts is almost solved! The submarine design will be found. Madame Andermatt's letters will be kept safe.

Thank you for your help, my dear sir.

Yours truly,
Salvator

I was very excited. I showed the letter to Jean Daspry. "Excellent!" he cried. "Let's hide in the library that night. I want to see what Salvator does."

I agreed. "We can hide behind the curtain. No one will see us there."

That night, Daspry and I hid in the library. At 8 o'clock, we heard a knock at the front door. Daspry looked surprised. "Someone is very early," he said.

I went to the door and opened it. It was Madame Andermatt.

"I must come in!" she cried. "I received a letter from Salvator. He said that I should come here. Tonight he will get my letters back!"

I brought Madame Andermatt into the library. Daspry greeted her politely.

"Welcome, madame," he said. "This may be an dangerous evening. Come stand behind the curtain with us. You will be safe here. Together we will watch and wait."

Suddenly we heard noises. Someone else had entered the house!

"Quiet!" Daspry said softly. "Do not say a word!"

Then a man entered the library. It was Alfred Varin. He walked slowly around the room. For a moment, I was afraid that he would find us.

But Varin did not look at the curtain. He looked at the paintings on the walls instead. Most of all, he looked at the painting of a strange old king. The king was dressed in red. He held a sword in his hands. The sword was covered with a design of red jewels.

Varin walked up to the painting of the king. He reached up to touch it. Suddenly there was a noise. Another person had entered the house. Varin moved quickly away from the painting.

"Who is there?" he cried.

Georges Andermatt entered the library. "I am here," he said. "Who is it?" Then he looked at Alfred Varin with surprise. An expression of hate

VI. The Seven of Hearts

covered his face. "Varin!" he said. "What are you doing here? I have nothing to say to a criminal like you!"

"I did not call you here," Varin said. "Something strange is happening. I don't like it. I will leave now."

Monsieur Andermatt stopped him. "Wait! I have one question for you, Varin! What have you done with Louis Lacombe? Tell me the truth!"

"I did nothing!" Varin cried. "He disappeared. My brother and I had nothing to do with that."

"You lie!" Monsieur Andermatt said. "You stole the design for the Seven of Hearts. You must have killed Louis Lacombe! Admit it!"

"I admit nothing," Varin answered. "Anyway, you cannot prove that. If you are sure of my guilt, why didn't you call the police?"

"You know why!" Monsieur Andermatt said. "You have those letters from my wife to Louis Lacombe. You threatened to publish them. You demanded that I stay silent."

Alfred Varin laughed. "Yes, I have the letters. You will never find them. They are hidden...hidden in this very room! But you will never get them."

Varin turned to go, but Andermatt held onto him. "I want those letters now!" he cried.

Varin reached into his pocket. He pulled out a gun!

Suddenly there was a shot, but it was not Varin. Varin's gun had dropped to the floor. I realized with surprise that Jean Daspry had fired the shot.

Varin cried out. "Who is there! Show yourself!"

Daspry jumped out from behind the curtain. He stopped Varin. "You won't murder anyone today," Daspry told him. Then he showed Varin the little metal card we had found in the garden. "Do you recognize this card? It was buried with the bones of Louis Lacombe."

Alfred Varin's face was white with fear. "Who are you?" he asked slowly.

Daspry did not answer. Instead, he turned to Monsieur Andermatt. "Good evening, monsieur," he said. "May I ask a few questions? Did you bring the piece of paper with Lacombe's secret details? The paper that explains the secrets of the submarine?"

"Yes, I brought it," Monsieur Andermatt said

VI. THE SEVEN OF HEARTS

slowly. "But why? Are you Salvator? Why have you brought us here?" He gave the piece of paper to Daspry.

Then Daspry looked at Varin. "Did you bring the submarine design? The design you stole from Louis Lacombe and sold to the Germans? Give it to me now." His strong voice was full of authority.

"Yes," Varin said. He had no choice. He gave the design to Daspry.

"Excellent!" said Daspry. "I have one more request for you, Varin. You must give back the letters of Madame Andermatt. They are hidden in this room… I know where they are. You know where they are. Get them now and give them to me." Then Daspry gave the metal card to Varin.

Varin walked to the painting of the red king. He put the metal card over the king's sword. The jewels in the king's sword matched the holes in the card. Varin pressed down. Suddenly the wall opened. A secret hiding place was revealed. The letters were inside.

Daspry took the letters. He gave them to Monsieur Andermatt. "Now I think you should go home, monsieur," he said. "Read those letters carefully! Do not judge your wife too quickly."

Monsieur Andermatt said goodbye and left.

Madame Andermatt and I were still behind the curtain. As Monsieur Andermatt took the letters, she fell against me. "I have no hope now!" she said softly. "My husband has my letters to Louis Lacombe. What will I do?" Her eyes closed. She had fainted, I realized!

Neither Jean Daspry nor Alfred Varin heard her. The two men stood in the middle of the room.

"You may go now, too" Daspry said to Varin.

"Not yet," Varin said. "You are the reason my brother Etienne killed himself. On June 22, you opened the secret hiding place. You took the money and jewels we had put there. You even took our secret papers! When my brother came to this house, he discovered that they were gone. That was why he killed himself!"

"I did take the money and jewels," Daspry said. "But they were never yours, Varin. You and your brother stole them! Now *I* am stealing them from you. How dare you complain? As for your papers, they reveal you to be a criminal and a murderer!"

VI. The Seven of Hearts

"Tell me your name," Varin said angrily. "Someday I will have my revenge on you! Tonight you have the victory... but there will come another time! I am your enemy now. Someday you will pay for your actions!"

Daspry laughed. "You want my name! Very well. I do not fear you, Varin. I am Salvator, but that is not my real name. When you do hear my real name, you will be even more afraid than you are now. My name is... *Arsène Lupin*."

Varin cried out in fear. "Lupin!" he said. He looked once into Daspry's face. Then he rushed out of the room.

I had been listening, too. I couldn't believe what I had heard. My friend Jean Daspry was actually Arsène Lupin, the famous gentleman-thief! I was in shock.

"It is safe now. You can come out," Daspry called.

I came out from behind the curtain. I brought Madame Andermatt with me. She had just woken up from her faint.

"Monsieur!" she cried. "The letters... you gave them to my husband! Why? What will I do?"

"Do not fear," Daspry told her. "Those were not the real letters. I took the real letters—your letters to Lacombe—out of the secret hiding place yesterday. Then I wrote some fake letters. Then I put them in the hiding place. Those fake letters are the ones I gave to your husband. When he reads them, he will discover that they are completely proper. He will never suspect you. He will love you again, madame."

Madame Andermatt was filled with joy. "Oh, thank you! Thank you!" she cried. "You have acted so kindly, monsieur. From now on, I will always be true to my husband. I will give him all of my love. Thank you for saving my marriage."

"I am glad to help," Daspry told her. "Goodbye, Madame Andermatt!"

After the lady had left, I looked at Daspry… or should I say Arsène Lupin?

"So now you know my secret!" Lupin said with a laugh. "Soon I will no longer use the name 'Jean Daspry.' I will only be Arsène Lupin."

"Thank you for trusting me," I said. "I am honored. What will you do next?"

"First, I will give the submarine plans to the French navy. The Seven of Hearts belongs to

VI. THE SEVEN OF HEARTS

France! Now that the plans are complete, the submarine can be built successfully. Then I will write a little newspaper article..."

The next day, this short article appeared in the *Echo de France*:

> *The Affair of the Seven of Hearts is over! Arsène Lupin has found the submarine plans for the Seven of Hearts. He has given these plans to the French navy. This great action is a victory for our country. Arsène Lupin may be a master thief, but he is also a noble citizen of France!*

That is the story of how I first met the great Arsène Lupin. Since then, I have been his friend. I have kept his secrets. He has described his many adventures to me. It is my pleasure to share them with you.

VII. Madame Imbert's Safe
アンベール夫人の金庫

【キーワード】
- [ ] struggle
- [ ] safe
- [ ] secretary
- [ ] force
- [ ] opportunity
- [ ] swindler

【あらすじと登場人物】

　暴漢から救出するという芝居をして信用させ、ちゃっかりと家に入り込むルパン。金庫から金を盗むことに成功したが……。

Ludovic Imbert　リュドビック＝アンベール　フランス一の金持ちと言われる。暴漢に襲われる。

VII.
Madame Imbert's Safe

This is the story of one of Arsène Lupin's earliest adventures. It is also one of the most strange. At the time when this adventure occurred, the name "Arsène Lupin" was not yet famous. In fact, this adventure marked the first time that our hero used the name.

* * *

The story begins one night in Paris. It was almost midnight. Monsieur Ludovic Imbert was returning home from a party. He walked alone on a quiet street.

Suddenly Monsieur Imbert heard a noise. He turned around and saw another man. The man was dressed all in black. He was walking along the street, too.

Imbert soon realized that he was being followed. He began to run. The man in black also began to run. Then he attacked Imbert, throwing him onto the ground. Imbert tried to struggle, but the man was too strong.

Then Imbert heard something else. "Stop!" a voice cried. "What are you doing? Leave that gentleman alone!" A young man had arrived on the scene.

This new arrival began to fight with the man in black. He pulled him up and hit the man in the face. With a cry of pain, the man in black ran away.

Imbert looked up. "Monsieur, you have saved me!" he cried. "That man attacked me. You have saved my life."

The young man smiled. "I am glad to help. How lucky that I happened to walk down this street!"

"Let me introduce myself. I am Ludovic

VII. Madame Imbert's Safe

Imbert. It is possible that you have heard of me," Imbert said.

"Yes, I have heard your name," the young man admitted.

Ludovic Imbert was famous. He was believed to be one of the richest men in France. Imbert and his wife had appeared in Paris a few years ago. Nobody knew where they came from, but they seemed very rich. The Imberts were famous for something else, too. Everyone in Paris knew that they did not keep their money in the bank. They kept all of their money in their house, in a large iron safe.

Imbert looked at the young man. He said, "What is your name? You must come to my house tomorrow. I would like to thank you. My wife will thank you, too."

"You are very kind," the young man said. "I will be glad to come to your house. My name is Arsène Lupin."

The two men shook hands and said goodbye. "Come to my house at 10 o'clock," Imbert said.

"I will be there!" Lupin answered.

* * *

Arsène Lupin returned home that night. He was very pleased. His plan was going well so far. The "attack" on Ludovic Imbert had not been real. Lupin himself had gotten someone to attack Imbert. Then Lupin had saved Imbert from the so-called attack.

"Now I have been invited to the Imberts' house," Lupin said to himself. "The next part of my plan begins… Soon the riches of Monsieur and Madame Imbert will be mine."

The next morning, Lupin went to the Imberts' house. It was large and beautiful. He knocked on the door.

Monsieur Imbert opened the door. He greeted Lupin warmly. "Come in!" he said. "I am glad to see you again. Please come and meet my wife."

Madame Imbert took Lupin's hand. "My dear Monsieur Lupin! My husband told me what happened last night. I can never thank you enough. You saved my husband's life!"

Arsène Lupin and the Imberts quickly became friends. Soon the Imberts realized that their new friend was poor. They offered to help him. They gave him a job in their house. Lupin became the Imberts' secretary. He wrote letters for them. He

VII. Madame Imbert's Safe

had an office in the house.

"My plan is going very well!" Lupin said to himself. "The Imberts trust me. They have let me into their house. Now I must find a way to break into their safe."

The safe was kept in the office of Madame Imbert. It was large, heavy, and made of iron. Lupin looked at the safe carefully.

"It is a very good, very strong safe," he thought. "It will be quite difficult to break into it. I cannot force it open. I must find another way... I will wait for the best opportunity."

That opportunity arrived several weeks later. Madame Imbert had gone to bed early. Monsieur Imbert was working in the office where the safe was kept. He had opened the safe and was counting the money.

Lupin came into the office. "Goodnight, Monsieur Imbert," he said. "I am going home now. But before I go, can I help you in any way?"

"Goodnight, my friend!" Imbert answered. "Thank you for asking. I do not need any help now. As you can see, I am just counting this money. I will be done in a few hours. See you tomorrow!"

Arsène Lupin said goodbye and closed the office door. He did not go home, however. Instead, he hid himself in the Imberts' house. He waited until everyone in the house (except Monsieur Imbert) was sleeping. Then he slipped silently into the office.

Monsieur Imbert sat at the desk. He was still counting the money. The safe was open. He did not hear Lupin enter the room. In an instant, Lupin had covered Imbert's eyes. Then he tied him up. Lupin did this with so much skill that Imbert was not hurt. Monsieur Imbert was not able to see Lupin's face, either.

Then Lupin took all the money out of the safe. He put it in a big bag. He closed the safe and left the office. He slipped out of the house and into the night. The theft was a success… The riches of Monsieur and Madame Imbert now belonged to Arsène Lupin!

The next day, a strange fact was reported in the newspapers. Monsieur and Madame Imbert had disappeared! No one ever saw them again.

* * *

VII. Madame Imbert's Safe

When Arsène Lupin finished telling me this story, he laughed. "I learned a lot from Monsieur and Madame Imbert," he said. "It was not a pleasant lesson, but I learned it."

"What do you mean?" I asked Lupin. "You succeeded! You took the money from the safe!"

"Yes, I took the money," Lupin said. "But that is not the end of the story."

"What happened?" I asked.

Lupin laughed again. Then he explained. "When I returned home that night, I took the money out of the bag. I began to count it," he said. "Soon I realized that something was wrong. It was not real money. It was all fake."

"The money was fake!" I cried. "So the Imberts were criminals!"

"Yes," said Lupin. "The Imberts were swindlers... They were not actually rich. They had fooled everyone in Paris with their fake money. They even fooled Arsène Lupin! It is the one time that I have been tricked... I promise you, my friend, that it will not happen again!"

VIII. The Black Pearl
黒真珠

【キーワード】
- [ ] approach
- [ ] average
- [ ] torn
- [ ] guilty
- [ ] locksmith
- [ ] fingerprint
- [ ] muddy
- [ ] dirt
- [ ] justice

【あらすじと登場人物】

アンジロ伯爵夫人宅から、「黒真珠」を盗もうと邸宅に侵入したルパン。が、そこにはすでに殺害された伯爵夫人の死体が。そして「黒真珠」も奪われていた。

Countess d'Andillot　アンジロ伯爵夫人

Captain Dudouis　デュドゥイ警察部長　ガニマール警部の上司。

Detective Ganimard　ガニマール警部　ルパン逮捕に執念を燃やす刑事。

Victor Danègre　ビクトール＝ダネーグル　伯爵夫人に仕える召使い。容疑者として逮捕される。

Anatole Dufour　アナトール＝デュフォール　ビクトール＝ダネーグルの偽名。

Grimaudan　グリモーダン　元国家警察部刑事の私立探偵。

VIII.
The Black Pearl

It was three o'clock in the morning. The streets of Paris were still dark. Arsène Lupin walked silently along the Avenue Hoche.

"It will be a fine day," he said to himself. "But now I have work to do!"

Lupin approached the house at 9 Avenue Hoche. It was the home of the Countess d'Andillot, owner of the famous black pearl. The Countess had received the pearl many years ago. It had been the gift of a king. It was her favorite jewel. She wore the pearl every day. At night, she kept it in a secret place in her bedroom.

Lupin examined the front door of the house. It was closed and locked. He laughed softly. He took a small tool out of his bag. He put it into the lock, and the door opened easily.

"So simple!" Lupin said to himself. "I already know where the Countess keeps the pearl. Soon it will be mine!"

He walked silently into the house. He found the door to the Countess's bedroom. The door was locked. With his skill, Lupin opened it easily. Then he entered the Countess's bedroom.

The room was dark and quiet. "The Countess sleeps well," Lupin thought. "She will not wake up easily. This job is almost too simple!" He moved carefully toward the table where the pearl was kept.

Suddenly, in the darkness, he felt something strange. Something was lying on the floor!

Arsène Lupin reached down. His hands touched something that was as cold as ice. He jumped back in surprise. Then he touched it again. It was a human face!

Quickly he turned on the lights. On the floor

VIII. The Black Pearl

lay a dead woman. She was covered in blood. She had many wounds. "It is the Countess!" Lupin said to himself. "She has been killed!"

A broken clock lay next to the dead Countess. The time on the clock was 11 p.m. "She was killed just a few hours ago," Lupin said. "The poor woman! Who would do such a terrible thing? And what did that person want?"

He hurried to the table. He searched for the pearl but could not find it. "The black pearl!" he said softly. "It has been stolen! Someone else knew about the secret hiding place!"

"I should leave," Lupin said to himself. "The scene of a murder is a dangerous place. I could get into trouble." But then he stopped. He thought for several minutes. "No, I will not leave yet," he decided. "An average man would leave. But not Arsène Lupin! I will stay here a while. I must study the crime. Then I will catch the thief...and get the black pearl, too."

* * *

The next morning, the crime was discovered.

When the Countess did not awake at the regular time, her servants knocked on the bedroom door. There was no answer. The door was locked. Finally, the servants broke down the door. Then they found the Countess's dead body.

The servants called the Paris police right away. Monsieur Dudouis, the captain of the police, came quickly. So did the famous Detective Ganimard. Captain Dudouis, Ganimard, and the police searched the Countess's bedroom. They looked at the broken clock. They spoke to the servants.

"The facts of the crime are clear," said Captain Dudouis. "The thief killed the Countess. He used a knife. Then he stole the black pearl. The broken clock tells us that the murder happened at 11 p.m. Also, the thief must have known the Countess well… He knew the secret place where she kept the pearl."

"Yes," agreed Ganimard. "But there is something even more important. I have just found a bit of cloth under the bed. It is covered with blood. The cloth does not belong to the Countess. It was torn from the criminal's clothing."

VIII. The Black Pearl

"Very good!" cried Dudouis. "If we can match the bit of cloth to the criminal's clothing, then we will catch him."

Ganimard looked thoughtful. "Perhaps," he said. "But that is not enough! Where is the knife that was used to kill the Countess? And how did the criminal enter the bedroom? The door was locked. Something is not quite right here. Too much evidence is missing... It is strange."

"My dear Ganimard!" Dudouis cried. "You are thinking too much. We have the bit of cloth. That is all we need!"

But Ganimard did not agree. "I wonder..." he said. "I wonder if Arsène Lupin is behind this."

"You think he murdered the Countess?" Dudouis asked.

"No, I do not accuse him of murder. In his own way, Lupin is a noble man. He would never have killed the Countess," said Ganimard. "But I wonder if he is interested in the black pearl."

Captain Dudouis laughed. "Ganimard, don't be a fool. You think that Lupin is behind every crime. You see him everywhere!"

Ganimard did not laugh. "Arsène Lupin is a

master thief," he told Dudouis. "If I see him everywhere, that is because he *is* everywhere."

* * *

The next day, Captain Dudouis arrested a man named Victor Danègre. He was a servant of the Countess. Danègre's coat matched the bit of bloody cloth that Ganimard had found. Dudouis put him in prison.

"I am certain that Danègre is guilty. He killed the Countess and stole the pearl," Captain Dudouis said.

"He probably is," Ganimard agreed. "But you do not have enough evidence."

Ganimard was right. The case against Victor Danègre was not strong. No one could prove that Danègre had the black pearl. The police searched his house, but the pearl was not there. Also, the police could not find the knife that had been used to kill the Countess. Finally, the police never proved that Danègre had a key to the Countess's bedroom.

Victor Danègre's trial was short. As Ganimard

VIII. THE BLACK PEARL

had said, there was not enough evidence. The judge did not find Danègre guilty. And so, six months after the Countess's death, Danègre was released from prison. He was a free man.

Victor Danègre was not happy, however. He was weak and tired after his time in prison. He changed his name to Anatole Dufour. He moved to a different part of Paris where no one knew him. He lived very quietly.

But Danègre did not feel safe. He felt as if he were being watched. "Someone is following me," he said to himself. "Someone is always watching me." He did not enjoy his life as a free man.

One night, Danègre was at a small restaurant. He was eating dinner alone. Then a strange man sat down at his table. He poured himself a glass of wine. "To your health, Victor Danègre," the man said.

Danègre was very afraid. But he decided to lie. "That is not my name," he said. "I am Anatole Dufour."

The man laughed. "Tell the truth! You are Victor Danègre. You were the servant of the Countess d'Andillot."

"Who are you?" Danègre asked.

"I am Monsieur Grimaudan. I used to work for the police. I was a detective. Now I work for myself," the man said.

"What do you want from me?" Danègre said.

"Your case interests me," Grimaudan told him. "I am especially interested in the black pearl."

"The black pearl?" Danègre said.

"Yes, the pearl you stole from the Countess."

"But I haven't got it," Danègre said. He tried to laugh. "If I had it, I would be the murderer!"

"You are the murderer. You killed the Countess," Grimaudan said calmly.

"No!" cried Danègre. "You are wrong! Even the judge agreed. He released me from prison. I am not guilty!"

Grimaudan smiled. He spoke softly. "Now listen to me, my friend. A week before the murder, you stole the key to the Countess's bedroom. You went to a locksmith named Outard. He made a copy of that key for you. That is how you entered the Countess's bedroom."

"That's a lie!" Danègre cried.

VIII. The Black Pearl

"Here is that key," Grimaudan said. He put the key on the table.

"You also bought a knife," Grimaudan said. "You bought it at the Bazaar de la Republique. You used that knife to kill the Countess."

"You cannot prove it!" Danègre said.

"Here is the knife," Grimaudan said. He put the knife on the table. "I have already spoken to the man who sold it to you. He remembers your face quite well."

"Is that all the evidence you have?" Danègre said. "It's not enough! No one will believe you!"

"There is one more thing," Grimaudan said calmly. "A very small thing…but very important, too."

"What are you talking about?" Danègre cried.

"You left a bloody fingerprint on the wall of the Countess's room. With that fingerprint, it will be quite easy to prove that you are guilty," Grimaudan told him.

Danègre was filled with fear. "Who are you? How do you know so much? What do you want from me?" he cried.

"I want the black pearl," Grimaudan answered.

"What will I get from you?" Danègre asked.

"You will not go to prison. You will be allowed to live. Is that not enough?" Grimaudan said. "You will give me the pearl now. You will show me where it is hidden."

Danègre knew that he was defeated. "Come with me," he said. "I will take you to the pearl."

The two men walked through the streets of Paris. Finally, they came to the Parc Monceau. Danègre pointed to the muddy street. "The black pearl is there," he said. "I put it in the dirt, between the stones."

"Show me which ones," Grimaudan said.

Danègre pointed to two large stones. He quickly dug between them. Then he pulled a small object out of the mud. It shone like a dark star. He handed it to Grimaudan.

"Here is the pearl," he said. "Now let me go!"

"Be off!" Grimaudan told him. "Be glad that you are escaping with your life!"

* * *

That is how Arsène Lupin got the famous black

VIII. The Black Pearl

pearl. Lupin told me the story himself.

"So Monsieur Grimaudan was actually you!" I said to Lupin.

"Yes," he said with a laugh. "It was better to play the part of Grimaudan. If I had told Victor Danègre that I was Arsène Lupin, he would have dropped dead from fear!"

Lupin smiled. Then he said, "But I am most proud of my efforts on the night of the Countess's death. I stayed in her bedroom and solved the crime. I searched the room. I quickly realized that the murderer was one of her servants. I found Danègre's key. Then I found his knife. When I discovered his bloody fingerprint on the wall, I had all the evidence I needed."

"So the police never noticed the fingerprint," I said.

"No, they did not," Lupin said. "The police never search very carefully, do they?"

"Why did you take Danègre's key and knife with you?" I asked Lupin. "Why did you leave the bloody bit of cloth at the scene of the crime?"

"I wanted the police to have enough evidence to suspect Danègre—but not to prove his guilt,"

Lupin explained. "Without the key and the knife, the case against Danègre was not strong enough. The judge had to set him free. After his time in prison, Danègre was weak and scared. Then it was easy to make him give me the pearl."

"The poor devil!" I said. "Victor Danègre never had a chance against you, Lupin."

"Do not feel sorry for him," Lupin told me. "He killed the Countess. It was right that I took the pearl from him. Justice has been done. As I said to Danègre, he is lucky to have escaped with his life."

IX. Shelock Holmes Arrives Too Late
遅かったホームズ

【キーワード】
- [ ] indeed
- [ ] eager
- [ ] figure
- [ ] admire
- [ ] respect
- [ ] delight
- [ ] worthy
- [ ] solution
- [ ] compliment

【あらすじと登場人物】
ティベルメニル城の宝を狙うルパン。だがこの城には秘密の通路があり、誰も通路への入り口を見つけることができない。城主は、有名なホームズに謎解きを依頼。そこで宿敵の2人が出会うことになる。

Georges Devanne ジョルジュ＝ドゥバンヌ ティベルメニル城の持ち主、大富豪。

Horace Velmont オラース＝ベルモン ドゥバンヌの友人で、ルパン似とからかわれる。

Sherlock Holmes シャーロック・ホームズ イギリスからやってきた有名な探偵。

Monsieur and Madame d'Androl アンドロル夫妻 ドゥバンヌの友人。

Mademoiselle Nelly ネリー嬢 アンドロル夫妻とともに夜中に城に到着した。

IX.
Sherlock Holmes Arrives Too Late

The Castle of Thibermesnil is one of the great castles of France. It is many hundreds of years old. Many kings of France have stayed here, including Louis XVI. The castle is also filled with many treasures.

A few years ago, a rich man named Georges Devanne bought the castle of Thibermesnil. At the time when this story occurred, Devanne had invited a large group of friends to stay at the castle for a week.

One night, Devanne and his guests were having dinner. Devanne was talking to one of his friends, Horace Velmont. Suddenly he stopped and smiled at him. "You look a bit like the famous Arsène Lupin," Devanne said. "It is quite surprising!"

Velmont laughed. "Many people have told me that," he answered. "Perhaps you should call the police, my dear Devanne!"

Devanne laughed, too. "Maybe you are right! After all, I have many fine paintings and other treasures in the castle. I'm sure that Arsène Lupin would like to steal them."

"Yes, Lupin would want to steal them," Velmont agreed with a smile. "Your treasures are very beautiful, indeed."

"Well, Lupin should hurry and steal them, if that is his plan," Devanne laughed. "After tonight, it will be much more difficult. Then my treasures will be safe... and I will sleep better!"

"Why is that?" another friend asked.

"A special guest is coming," Devanne told the group. "He arrives tomorrow at 4 o'clock. You will never guess his name, so I will tell you. He is Sherlock Holmes!"

Everyone became very excited. "Sherlock Holmes! The famous English detective! But why is he coming?" they asked.

Georges Devanne looked serious. "I believe that Arsène Lupin will try to steal my treasures. So I wrote to Sherlock Holmes. I explained the situation to him. Monsieur Holmes wrote back quickly. He said that he was glad to come. He is eager to catch the famous Arsène Lupin."

"The greatest detective will face the greatest thief in the world!" Velmont said. "How exciting! Finally, Arsène Lupin will have an enemy who is his equal. This will be interesting."

"Why do you think Lupin wants to steal your treasures?" another friend asked Devanne.

"Strange things have happened recently," Devanne said. "Someone stole a special book from my private library. This book was very old. It contains the plans for the castle. The plans show exactly how the castle was built. They show every entrance and exit. The plans also mention a secret tunnel into the castle."

"A secret tunnel into the castle! Where is it?" Velmont asked.

"I do not know," Devanne said. "No one knows exactly where the tunnel is. The plans do not describe the exact location. The only thing we know is that the tunnel entrance is somewhere in this room."

Everyone looked around the large and beautiful room. It was the oldest room in the castle. It was filled with fine paintings and other treasures. A large bookcase covered one wall of the room. The word "Thibermesnil" was written in big gold letters at the top.

"I have searched this room," Devanne told his friends. "But I cannot find the tunnel entrance! That is why I have called Sherlock Holmes. He

IX. Sherlock Holmes Arrives Too Late

will solve the mystery. He will find the secret tunnel. Then he will stop Arsène Lupin from stealing my treasures!"

"Is the secret tunnel mentioned in any history books? This castle is very old," Velmont said.

"Actually, the tunnel was used by King Louis XVI," said Devanne. "He visited the castle as a guest. The king even mentioned the tunnel in his diary. But he never explained how he entered the tunnel. He wrote only one sentence about it. It is very strange."

"What did he write?" Velmont asked. "Tell us!"

"The king wrote this sentence: 'Turn one eye on the bee that shakes, and the other eye will lead to God!' It makes no sense at all. I cannot figure out what it means," Devanne said. "Sherlock Holmes will solve this mystery, though."

"Perhaps," said Velmont quietly. "Or maybe Arsène Lupin will solve it first!"

Dinner was now finished. "It is getting late," Devanne said. "My guests, you must excuse me. Three more friends are arriving on the midnight train. I will leave you now. I must drive to the train station and meet them." He said goodnight and left.

The other guests said goodnight, too. They left the dining room and went to bed.

At 1 a.m., Devanne returned from the train station. With him were Monsieur and Madame d'Androl and a young lady who was a friend of theirs. They were tired after their journey and soon went to bed, too.

By 3 a.m., the castle was quiet and dark. Everyone was asleep. No one heard three soft noises. They sounded like a key being turned in a lock. The noises came from the oldest room of the castle.

Suddenly the bookcase in the room began to move. It opened like a door. Behind it was the secret tunnel. Three men walked quietly into the room. One of them was Arsène Lupin.

"We do not have much time," Lupin said to his two helpers. "Take the paintings off the wall. Carry them into the tunnel. Bring them back to the car. Take them to my house. I will stay here. Do not wait for me."

The two helpers quickly took the paintings. They brought them into the secret tunnel. Lupin pushed the bookcase back into its normal place.

Then he walked to a glass-covered case in the

IX. Sherlock Holmes Arrives Too Late

center of the room. The case was full of jewels. Lupin opened the case and began to steal the jewels.

Suddenly he heard a sound. Someone was walking toward the room! Someone was about to come in!

Lupin hid behind a curtain. He waited silently. Then he heard the door open. Someone had entered the room. Then he heard a woman's voice. "Who is it?" the woman asked softly. "Who is there?"

"I know that voice!" Arsène Lupin thought to himself. "I remember that sweet voice. But it cannot be! It is impossible!"

Suddenly the woman moved the curtain. She stood face to face with Lupin. It was Mademoiselle Nelly! Her beautiful face was white with shock.

"It is you, Mademoiselle Nelly!" Lupin cried. "What are you doing here?"

"I...I arrived tonight," she said slowly. "I came on the midnight train. Monsieur Devanne met us at the train station." She looked into Lupin's eyes. Then she looked around the room. She saw that he had stolen the paintings and the jewels. Her face changed.

"See how she looks at me," Lupin thought to himself. "She sees me as a thief, nothing more. She does not care for me."

Suddenly he put down the jewels. Then he looked at Mademoiselle Nelly. "I am sorry, Mademoiselle," he said. "For you, I will return everything. All the paintings will be returned. Tomorrow I will bring back everything that I have taken. I promise this to you. Everything will be returned tomorrow, at 3 o'clock. You have my promise."

Mademoiselle Nelly looked into Lupin's eyes again. "Tomorrow at 3 o'clock?" she said. "But how? You will be caught! The police will be here. It is too dangerous. You must not do it!"

"I have made a promise to you," Lupin said. "I will keep that promise, Mademoiselle." Then he disappeared into the night.

* * *

In the morning, Georges Devanne discovered the thefts. "Arsène Lupin has been here!" he cried. "I knew he would come."

IX. Sherlock Holmes Arrives Too Late

Devanne called the police. They quickly arrived. They searched the castle, but they found nothing. There was no sign of Lupin anywhere.

"Lupin must have used the secret tunnel," Devanne said. "If only Sherlock Holmes had been here yesterday... He would have found the tunnel. He would have stopped Lupin! Luckily, Monsieur Holmes will arrive today."

Horace Velmont entered the room. "My dear Devanne," he said. "I am sorry about the thefts. It must have been Arsène Lupin."

"Yes, I think so," Devanne answered. He laughed and said, "I should tell the police about you, my friend. You look so much like Lupin! I'm sure the police would find it funny!"

Velmont laughed, too. "Yes indeed! It is very funny."

Then Mademoiselle Nelly came into the room. She looked at Velmont. She almost cried out in surprise. Georges Devanne saw her shock.

"Do not worry, Mademoiselle Nelly," Devanne said with a smile. "This is my friend, Monsieur Velmont. He looks like Arsène Lupin, I know—but do not fear! He is not the famous gentleman-thief."

Velmont bowed. "It is a pleasure to meet you," he said.

Mademoiselle Nelly did not speak, but she let Velmont take her arm. They walked to a window. No one heard their conversation.

"What are you doing here?" she said softly. "You will be caught!"

"No, Mademoiselle," he answered. "I will not be caught. Anyway, I have a promise to keep. Remember what I said. Today at 3 o'clock, I will return everything that was stolen." He bowed again and walked away.

The day passed quickly. Mademoiselle Nelly watched the clock. Soon it was almost 3 o'clock. How would Lupin keep his promise?

At exactly 3 o'clock, there was a knock at the gates of the castle. A servant rushed to find Georges Devanne. "Monsieur Devanne," he said. "Please come quickly! Everything that was stolen has been returned!"

Devanne and his guests hurried to the front gates. A large wagon was there. The wagon was filled with all the treasures of the castle. "Lupin has returned everything!" Devanne cried. "How strange! He is truly a gentleman-thief."

IX. Sherlock Holmes Arrives Too Late

Mademoiselle Nelly was amazed. She looked at the wagon. Then she looked at Horace Velmont—at Arsène Lupin. Her beautiful eyes shone.

Lupin looked at her and gave a small smile. "I have kept my promise," he said softly. "Now I must say goodbye again, my dear mademoiselle."

Lupin left the castle quietly. He walked through the gardens. As he walked, he met another man going toward the castle.

"Excuse me," the man said. "Is this the way to the castle?" He spoke in French, but his voice sounded English.

"You are correct," said Lupin. "The castle is very close. Monsieur Devanne is expecting you, Monsieur Holmes."

"Ah! You know my name."

"Yes. Last night, my friend Devanne told us that you were coming. I am happy to meet you," Lupin said. "No one in France admires Sherlock Holmes more than I do." He smiled strangely.

Holmes looked at Lupin closely. His sharp eyes studied Lupin's face. It was a historic moment. The greatest detective in the world and the greatest thief faced each other silently. Although

Holmes and Lupin were enemies, each had respect for the other.

"Thank you, monsieur," Holmes said. "I hope... we meet again."

"I am certain that we will," Lupin answered.

The two men bowed. Then they continued on their separate ways. Holmes went to the castle, and Lupin walked toward the train station.

When Sherlock Holmes arrived at the castle, Georges Devanne greeted him. "Monsieur Holmes, welcome! I am delighted to meet you. Thank you for coming... However, there is nothing for you to do here."

"What do you mean?" Holmes asked.

"Arsène Lupin found the secret tunnel last night," Devanne said. "He stole my treasures. But strangely, he has just returned them! So there is no crime to be solved now."

"Perhaps," said Holmes. "But what about the secret tunnel? Have you discovered where it is?"

"No," said Devanne. "Can you find it?"

"Of course," answered Holmes. "But first, you must tell me exactly what happened last night. Tell me everything."

Devanne described the entire evening. He

IX. Sherlock Holmes Arrives Too Late

repeated the conversation with Velmont. Sherlock Holmes listened carefully. When Devanne told the story of King Louis XVI and the strange sentence, Holmes smiled.

"That is how Lupin discovered the tunnel," Holmes said. "He has solved the secret of the sentence: 'Turn one eye on the bee that shakes, and the other eye will lead to God.'"

"So my friend Horace Velmont is actually Arsène Lupin!" Devanne cried. "I should have guessed."

"Yes, Velmont is Lupin," Holmes said. "I met him earlier, in fact. He was leaving the castle just as I was arriving."

"You met Lupin?" Devanne cried. "Why didn't you arrest him?"

"That is not how I work," Holmes said proudly. "Lupin is a worthy enemy. He figured out how to open the tunnel. That is how he took the stolen objects out of the castle."

"Can you figure out how to open the tunnel, too?" Devanne asked Holmes.

"If Lupin can do it, so can I," Holmes answered. "Give me one hour. I will think. Then I will have the solution."

For exactly one hour, Holmes sat and thought. He searched the room where the theft had occurred. Then a light came into his eyes. "I have the answer," he said to Devanne. "Look at the bookcase. Do you see the word 'Thibermesnil' above it?"

"Yes, 'Thibermesnil' is written in gold letters," Devanne said. "Why is that important?"

"Watch," said Holmes. He stood on a chair so that he could reach the gold letters. First, he touched the first "I" in "Thibermesnil." He moved the letter backward and forward. Next, he touched the letter "B" and moved it, too. Finally, he moved the last letter "I" in the word. As Sherlock Holmes moved each letter, a soft noise could be heard.

Suddenly the bookcase itself began to move. It opened like a door. Behind it was the secret tunnel.

"Amazing!" said Devanne. "But I don't understand. How did you figure it out?"

"The answer was simple," Holmes said. "The sentence explains it: 'Turn one eye on the bee that shakes, and the other eye will lead to God.' It is a play on words. The 'eye' in the sentence is the

IX. Sherlock Holmes Arrives Too Late

letter 'I,' and the 'bee' is the letter 'B.'"

"But what does the rest of the sentence mean?" Devanne asked. "How does the tunnel lead to God?"

"We will soon see," Holmes answered. "Let us go into the tunnel. We will see where it leads."

Devanne and Sherlock Holmes walked into the tunnel. It was dark and cold. They walked for ten minutes. Finally they saw a bit of light.

"We are almost at the end of the tunnel," Holmes said.

"But where are we?" Devanne asked.

"I have an idea," said Holmes. "I believe that we are in the church near the castle. Let us see."

They walked out of the tunnel. They found themselves in the church, as Holmes had said.

"So this is how Arsène Lupin escaped!" cried Devanne.

"Yes, this is how Lupin took the treasures from the castle," said Holmes. "This also explains the strange sentence. The tunnel leads to a church. In other words, the tunnel leads to God."

Devanne looked out of the church window. He saw a car waiting outside. "That is my car and driver!" he said. "Why are they here?"

Devanne and Holmes rushed outside. Devanne spoke to the driver of the car. "Why are you here?" Devanne asked. "I did not ask you to meet us here. Who sent you here?"

"It was Monsieur Velmont," the driver said. "He told me to meet you here, Monsieur Devanne. He said that you and Sherlock Holmes would be here at the church."

"Monsieur Velmont?" cried Devanne. "But he is Arsène Lupin!"

Sherlock Holmes smiled. "It is a compliment," he told Devanne.

"What do you mean?" asked Devanne.

"Arsène Lupin knew that I would figure out the secret. He knew that I would find the tunnel. That is why he sent your car here," Holmes explained. "Lupin is a worthy enemy. Now my work is done here. I will return to the train station and go back to England."

Devanne and Holmes got into the car. The driver took them toward the train station.

As they drove, Devanne noticed a letter in the car. It was addressed to Sherlock Holmes. "This letter is for you," Devanne said. "It must be from Lupin!"

IX. SHERLOCK HOLMES ARRIVES TOO LATE

Holmes opened the letter. Inside the letter was a watch. "That is my watch," he said. "Lupin must have stolen it!" His face grew dark with anger.

Georges Devanne suddenly laughed. "Arsène Lupin stole the watch of the great Sherlock Holmes! Now he is returning it! I am sorry for laughing, Monsieur Holmes. You must excuse me, but it is very funny. You must admit that Lupin is a master thief!"

But Sherlock Holmes did not laugh. "Yes, he is a master thief. But I am the greatest detective in the world. Someday Arsène Lupin and I will meet again. Then we will see who is the best..."

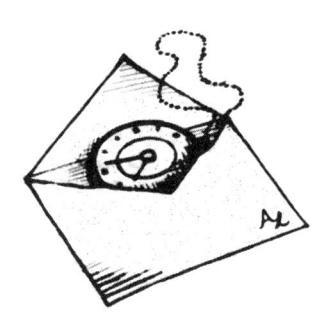

Word List

- 本文で使われている全ての語を掲載しています（LEVEL 1、2）。ただし、LEVEL 3 以上は、中学校レベルの語を含みません。
- 語形が規則変化する語の見出しは原形で示しています。不規則変化語は本文中で使われている形になっています。
- 一般的な意味を紹介していますので、一部の語で本文で実際に使われている品詞や意味と合っていないことがあります。
- 品詞は以下のように示しています。

名 名詞	代 代名詞	形 形容詞	副 副詞	動 動詞	助動 助動詞
前 前置詞	接 接続詞	間 間投詞	冠 冠詞	略 略語	俗 俗語
頭 接頭語	尾 接尾語	記 記号	関 関係代名詞		

A

- **about to** 熟《be –》まさに〜しようとしている、〜するところだ
- **accept** 動 ①受け入れる ②同意する、認める
- **according** 副《– to 〜》〜によれば［よると］
- **accuse** 動《– of 〜》〜（の理由）で告訴［非難］する
- **act** 動 行動する
- **active** 形 ①活動的な ②積極的な
- **actually** 副 実際に、本当に、実は
- **address** 名 住所、アドレス 動 ①あて名を書く ②演説をする、話しかける
- **admire** 動 感心する、賞賛する
- **admit** 動 認める、許可する、入れる
- **adventure** 名 冒険
- **affair** 名 ①事柄、事件 ②《-s》業務、仕事、やるべきこと
- **after a while** しばらくして
- **after all** やはり、結局
- **afterwards** 副 その後、のちに
- **ah** 間《驚き・悲しみ・賞賛などを表して》ああ、やっぱり
- **aha** 間 はあ、なるほど
- **Alfred Varin** アルフレッド＝バラン《人名》
- **all** 熟 **after all** やはり、結局 **most of all** とりわけ、中でも **not 〜 at all** 少しも［全然］〜ない
- **allow** 動 ①許す、《– … to 〜》…が〜するのを可能にする、…に〜させておく ②与える
- **alone** 熟 **leave 〜 alone** 〜をそっとしておく
- **although** 接 〜だけれども、〜にもかかわらず、たとえ〜でも
- **amazed** 形 びっくりした、驚いた
- **amazing** 形 驚くべき、見事な
- **ambassador** 名 大使、使節
- **America** 名 アメリカ《国名・大陸》
- **Anatole Dufour** アナトール＝デュフォール《人名》
- **Andermatt, Georges** ジョルジュ＝アンデルマット《人名》
- **Andermatt, Madame** アンデルマット夫人
- **anger** 名 怒り
- **angrily** 副 怒って、腹立たしげに
- **announce** 動（人に）知らせる、公

Word List

- **anyone** 代 ①《疑問文・条件節で》誰か ②《否定文で》誰も(〜ない) ③《肯定文で》誰でも
- **anyway** 副 ①いずれにせよ、ともかく ②どんな方法でも
- **anywhere** 副 どこかへ[に]、どこにも、どこへも、どこにでも
- **appear** 動 ①現れる、見えてくる ②(〜のように)見える、〜らしい appear to するように見える
- **appearance** 名 ①現れること、出現 ②外見、印象
- **approach** 動 接近する
- **arrest** 動 逮捕する 名 逮捕
- **arrival** 名 ①到着 ②到達
- **Arsène Lupin** アルセーヌ=ルパン
- **art** 熟 work of art 芸術品
- **article** 名 (新聞・雑誌などの)記事、論文
- **as** 熟 as for 〜に関しては、〜はどうかと言うと as if あたかも〜のように、まるで〜みたいに see 〜 as … 〜を…と考える
- **asleep** 形 眠って(いる状態の) fall asleep 眠り込む、寝入る
- **attack** 動 ①襲う、攻める ②非難する 名 攻撃、非難
- **attend** 動 出席する
- **attention** 名 ①注意、集中 ②配慮、手当て、世話
- **author** 名 著者、作家
- **authority** 名 権威、権力、権限
- **Avenue Hoche** オッシュ通り
- **average** 形 平均の、普通の
- **awake** 動 ①目覚めさせる ②目覚める 形 目が覚めて
- **awoke** 動 awake (目覚めさせる) の過去

B

- **backward** 副 後方へ、逆に、後ろ向きに backward and forward 前後に
- **badly** 副 ①悪く、まずく、へたに ②とても、ひどく
- **ball** 名 (大)舞踏会
- **banker** 名 銀行家[員]
- **Baron** 名 男爵
- **Baron Nathan Cahorn** ナタン=カオルン男爵
- **Batignolles** 名 バティニョル《地名、駅名》
- **Baudru, Désiré** デジレ=ボードリュ《人名》
- **Bazaar de la République** レピュブリック広場の市場
- **beauty** 名 美
- **bedroom** 名 寝室
- **bee** 名 ミツバチ
- **beggar** 名 乞食、物貰い
- **beginning** 名 初め、始まり
- **behind** 前 〜の後ろに、〜の背後に 副 後ろに、背後に
- **belief** 名 信じること、信念、信用
- **belong** 動 《− to 〜》〜に属する、〜のものである
- **below** 副 下に[へ]
- **Berlat, Guillaume** ギョーム=ベルラ《人名》
- **Bernard d'Andrézy** ベルナール=ダンドレジ《人名》
- **bit** 名 ①小片、少量 ②《a −》少し、ちょっと
- **blackmail** 動 脅迫する、ゆする
- **blame** 動 とがめる、非難する
- **blood** 名 ①血、血液 ②血統、家柄 ③気質
- **bloody** 形 血だらけの、血なまぐさい、むごい

The Adventures of Arsène Lupin, Gentleman-Thief

- □ **blow** 名打撃
- □ **board** 動乗り込む
- □ **bone** 名骨
- □ **bookcase** 名本箱
- □ **bottom** 名①底, 下部, すそ野, ふもと, 最下位, 根元 ②尻 形底の, 根底の
- □ **Boulevard Maillot** マイヨー通り
- □ **bow** 動(~に)お辞儀する
- □ **break into** ~に押し入る, 入り込む
- □ **breathe** 動呼吸する
- □ **Bridge Saint Michel** サン＝ミシェル橋
- □ **bring back** 戻す, 呼び戻す, 持ち帰る
- □ **British** 形①英国人の ②イギリス英語の 名英国人
- □ **bury** 動埋葬する, 埋める
- □ **businessmen** 名 businessman (ビジネスマン) の複数
- □ **but** 熟 not ~ but … ~ではなくて…

C

- □ **cabin** 名船室, キャビン
- □ **café** 名コーヒー[喫茶]店, 軽食堂
- □ **Cahorn, Baron Nathan** ナタン＝カオルン男爵
- □ **call for** ~を求める, 訴える, ~を呼び求める, 呼び出す
- □ **calm** 形穏やかな, 落ち着いた
- □ **calmly** 副落ち着いて, 静かに
- □ **camera** 名カメラ
- □ **can hardly** とても~できない
- □ **cannot** can (~できる) の否定形 (=can not)
- □ **captain** 名長, 船長, 首領, 主将
- □ **Captain Dudouis** デュドゥイ国家警察部部長
- □ **care for** ~の世話をする, ~を扱う, ~が好きである, ~を大事に思う
- □ **carry into** ~の中に運び入れる
- □ **cell** 名独房
- □ **certain** 形①確実な, 必ず~する ②(人が)確信した ③ある ④いくらかの
- □ **certainly** 副①確かに, 必ず ②《返答に用いて》もちろん, そのとおり, 承知しました
- □ **chance** 熟 by chance 偶然, たまたま
- □ **chase** 動①追跡する, 追い[探し]求める ②追い立てる
- □ **check** 動照合する, 検査する
- □ **chest** 名①大きな箱, 戸棚, たんす ②金庫
- □ **Chevalier** 名勲爵士, ナイト《称号》
- □ **Chevalier Floriani** フロニアー二勲爵士
- □ **choice** 名選択(の範囲・自由), えり好み, 選ばれた人[物]
- □ **cigar** 名葉巻
- □ **citizen** 名①市民, 国民 ②住民, 民間人
- □ **claim** 動①主張する ②要求する, 請求する
- □ **clear** 形①はっきりした, 明白な ②澄んだ ③(よく)晴れた
- □ **clearly** 副①明らかに, はっきりと ②《返答に用いて》そのとおり
- □ **clicking sound** カチッという音
- □ **closed** 形閉じた, 閉鎖した
- □ **closely** 副①密接に ②念入りに, 詳しく ③ぴったりと
- □ **clothing** 名衣類, 衣料品
- □ **clue** 名手がかり, 糸口
- □ **coast** 名海岸, 沿岸
- □ **come out** 出てくる, 姿を現す

Word List

- **complain** 動 ①不平 [苦情] を言う, ぶつぶつ言う ②(病状などを)訴える
- **complete** 形 完全な, まったくの, 完成した
- **completely** 副 完全に, すっかり
- **compliment** 名 賛辞, 敬意
- **conduct** 動 ①指導する ②実施する, 処理 [処置] する
- **conductor** 名 指導者, 案内者, 管理者, 指揮者, 車掌
- **confidence** 名 自信, 確信, 信頼, 信用度
- **confused** 形 困惑した, 混乱した
- **contain** 動 ①含む, 入っている ②(感情などを) 抑える
- **control** 名 ①管理, 支配(力) ②抑制 in control ～を支配して, ～を掌握している
- **conversation** 名 会話, 会談
- **copy** 名 ①コピー, 写し ②(書籍の)一部, 冊 ③広告文
- **correct** 形 正しい, 適切な, りっぱな
- **correctly** 副 正しく, 正確に
- **could** 熟 could have done ～だったかもしれない《仮定法》 How could ～? 何だって～なんてことがありえようか?
- **count** 名 伯爵 動 数える
- **Count Dreux-Soubise** ドルー=スービーズ伯爵
- **countess** 名 伯爵婦人
- **Countess d'Andillot** アンジロ伯爵夫人
- **Countess Dreux-Soubise** ドルー=スービーズ伯爵夫人
- **countryside** 名 地方, 田舎
- **courthouse** 名 裁判所
- **courtyard** 名 中庭
- **cover** 動 覆う, 包む, 隠す
- **crash** 名 ①激突, 墜落 ②(壊れるときの)すさまじい音
- **create** 動 創造する, 生み出す, 引き起こす
- **crime** 名 ①(法律上の)罪, 犯罪 ②悪事, よくない行為
- **criminal** 名 犯罪者, 犯人
- **crowd** 名 群集, 雑踏, 多数, 聴衆
- **d'Andillot, Countess** アンジロ伯爵夫人
- **d'Andrézy, Bernard** ベルナール=ダンドレジー《人名》
- **d'Androl, Monsieur and Madame** アンドロル夫妻

D

- **Danègre, Victor** ビクトール=ダネーグル《人名》
- **dare** 動《 – to ～》思い切って [あえて] ～する 助 思い切って [あえて] ～する How dare you ～! よくも～できるね.
- **darkness** 名 暗さ, 暗やみ
- **Daspry, Jean** ジャン=ダスプリ《人名》
- **day** 熟 one day (過去の) ある日, (未来の) いつか
- **de** 前《フランス語の前置詞で, 英語のofに相当》
- **deal** 名 取引
- **death** 名 死, 死ぬこと
- **defeat** 動 打ち破る, 負かす
- **definitely** 副 ①限定的に, 明確に, 確実に ②まったくそのとおり
- **delight** 動 喜ぶ, 喜ばす, 楽しむ, 楽しませる 名 喜び, 愉快
- **Delivet, Officer** ドリベ刑事
- **demand** 動 ①要求する, 尋ねる ②必要とする
- **depend** 動《 – on [upon] ～》①～

を頼る, ～をあてにする ②～による
- **describe** 動 (言葉で) 描写する, 特色を述べる, 説明する
- **description** 名 (言葉で) 記述 (すること), 描写 (すること)
- **design** 動 設計する, 企てる 名 デザイン, 設計 (図)
- **desire** 動 強く望む, 欲する
- **Désiré Baudru** デジレ＝ボードリュ《人名》
- **destroy** 動 破壊する, 絶滅させる, 無効にする
- **detail** 名 細部, 《-s》詳細
- **detective** 名 探偵, 刑事
- **Detective Ganimard** ガニマール警部
- **determine** 動 ①決心する [させる] ②決定する [させる]
- **Devanne, Georges** ジョルジュ＝ドゥバンヌ《人名》
- **device** 名 装置
- **diary** 名 日記
- **dig** 動 掘る
- **dine** 動 食事をする, ごちそうする
- **dining room** ダイニングルーム, 食堂
- **dirt** 名 ①汚れ, 泥, ごみ ②土
- **disappear** 動 見えなくなる, 姿を消す, なくなる
- **disappoint** 動 失望させる, がっかりさせる
- **disappointed** 形 がっかりした, 失望した
- **discovery** 名 発見
- **discuss** 動 議論 [検討] する
- **disguise** 名 変装 (すること)
- **do with** ～を処理する
- **doubt** 名 疑い, 不確かなこと **no doubt** きっと, たぶん
- **dressed** 形 服を着た

- **Dreux-Soubise, Count** ドルー＝スービーズ伯爵
- **Dreux-Soubise, Countess** ドルー＝スービーズ伯爵夫人
- **drive away** 車で走り去る
- **drive back to** 車で～に戻る
- **drive into** 車で～に突っ込む
- **driver** 名 ①運転手 ②(馬車の) 御者
- **drove** 動 drive (車で行く) の過去
- **drug** 動 (人) に薬を盛る [一服盛る]
- **Du Barry, Madame** デュ・バリー夫人
- **Dudouis, Captain** デュドゥイ国家警察部部長
- **dug** 動 dig (掘る) の過去, 過去分詞

E

- **each other** お互いに
- **eager** 形 ①熱心な ②《be－for ～》～を切望している, 《be－to ～》しきりに～したがっている
- **easily** 副 ①容易に, たやすく, 苦もなく ②気楽に
- **Echo de France** エコー・ド・フランス《新聞名》
- **effect** 名 影響, 効果, 結果
- **effort** 名 努力 (の成果)
- **elegance** 名 優雅さ, 上品さ
- **else** 熟 **no one else** 他の誰一人として～しない **or else** さもないと
- **enemy** 名 敵
- **England** 名 ①イングランド ②英国
- **entire** 形 全体の, 完全な, まったくの
- **equal** 名 同等のもの [人]
- **escape** 動 逃げる, 免れる, もれる
- **Etienne Varin** エティエンヌ＝バ

WORD LIST

ラン《人名》
- **everyone** 代 誰でも, 皆
- **everything** 代 すべてのこと[もの], 何でも, 何もかも
- **everywhere** 副 どこにいても, いたるところに
- **evidence** 名 ①証拠, 証人 ②形跡
- **exact** 形 正確な, 厳密な, きちょうめんな
- **examine** 動 試験する, 調査[検査]する, 診察する
- **excellent** 形 優れた, 優秀な
- **except** 前 ～を除いて, ～のほかは
- **excited** 形 興奮した, わくわくした
- **excitement** 名 興奮(すること)
- **exciting** 形 興奮させる, わくわくさせる
- **exercise** 名 ①運動, 体操 ②練習
- **exist** 動 存在する, 生存する, ある, いる
- **exit** 名 出口
- **expect** 動 予期[予測]する, (当然のこととして)期待する
- **expression** 名 ①表現, 表示, 表情 ②言い回し, 語句
- **extremely** 副 非常に, 極度に

F

- **face to face** 面と向かって
- **fact** 熟 in fact つまり, 実は, 要するに
- **fail** 動 失敗する
- **faint** 動 気絶する 名 気絶, 失神
- **fake** 動 見せかける, でっち上げる, だます, 偽造する 名 にせもの
- **fall asleep** 眠り込む, 寝入る
- **fall in love** 恋におちる
- **fall over** ～につまずく, ～の上に倒れかかる
- **fall to the ground** 転ぶ
- **fallen** 動 fall (落ちる) の過去分詞
- **far** 熟 far away 遠く離れて so far 今までのところ, これまでは
- **fear** 名 ①恐れ ②心配, 不安 in fear おどおどして, ビクビクして with fear 怖がって 動 ①恐れる ②心配する
- **feel better** 気分がよくなる
- **feel sick** 気分が悪い
- **feel sorry for** ～をかわいそうに思う
- **feeling** 名 ①感じ, 気持ち ②触感, 知覚 ③同情, 思いやり, 感受性
- **fight with** ～と戦う
- **figure** 動 ①描写する, 想像する ②計算する ③目立つ, (～として)現れる figure out 理解する, ～であるとわかる, (原因などを)解明する
- **filled** 形 一杯詰まった
- **final** 形 最後の, 決定的な
- **find out** 見つけ出す, 気がつく, 知る, 調べる, 解明する
- **fingerprint** 名 指紋
- **first-class** 形 (乗り物の)一等の
- **fit** 動 合致[適合]する, 合致させる
- **fix** 動 ①固定する[させる] ②修理する ③決定する ④用意する, 整える
- **Floriani, Chevalier** フロニアーニ勲爵士
- **fool** 名 ①ばか者, おろかな人 ②道化師 動 ばかにする, だます, ふざける
- **foot** 熟 on foot 歩いて
- **footprint** 名 足型, 足跡
- **force** 動 強制する, 力ずくで～する, 余儀なく～させる
- **forgive** 動 許す, 免除する
- **forward** 副 ①前方に ②将来に向けて ③先へ, 進んで backward and

THE ADVENTURES OF ARSÈNE LUPIN, GENTLEMAN-THIEF

forward 前後に
- □ **franc** フラン《フランスの旧通貨単位》
- □ **France** 名フランス《国名》
- □ **free** 熟 free will 自由意志 go free 自由の身になる set free (人)を解放する, 釈放される, 自由の身になる
- □ **French** 形フランス(人・語)の 名①フランス語 ②《the –》フランス人
- □ **friendship** 名友人であること, 友情
- □ **from now on** 今後
- □ **fun** 熟 have fun 楽しむ
- □ **funny** 形①おもしろい, こっけいな ②奇妙な, うさんくさい
- □ **furniture** 名家具, 備品, 調度

G

- □ **Ganimard, Detective** ガニマール警部
- □ **generous** 形①寛大な, 気前のよい ②豊富な
- □ **Georges Andermatt** ジョルジュ＝アンデルマット《人名》
- □ **Georges Devanne** ジョルジュ＝ドゥバンヌ《人名》
- □ **German** 名ドイツ人 形ドイツ(人)の
- □ **get** 熟 get ~ back ~を取り返す[戻す] get away 逃げる, 逃亡する, 離れる get in 中に入る, 乗り込む get into ~に入る, 入り込む get into trouble 面倒を起こす, 困った事になる, トラブルに巻き込まれる get out 外に出る, 出て行く get ready 用意[支度]をする get someone to do (人)に~させる[してもらう] get up 起き上がる, 立ち上がる have got 持っている
- □ **gift** 名①贈り物 ②(天賦の)才能
- □ **give back** (~を)返す
- □ **give up** あきらめる, やめる, 引き渡す
- □ **glad to do** 《be –》~してうれしい, 喜んで~する
- □ **gladly** 副喜んで, うれしそうに
- □ **glass-covered** 形ガラス張りの
- □ **go away** 立ち去る
- □ **go free** 自由の身になる
- □ **gold** 名金, 金貨, 金製品, 金色 形金の, 金製の, 金色の
- □ **goodnight** 間《就寝時・夜の別れ》おやすみ
- □ **gotten** 動 get (得る)の過去分詞
- □ **grateful** 形感謝する, ありがたく思う
- □ **greet** 動①あいさつする ②(喜んで)迎える
- □ **Grimaudan** 名グリモーダン《人名》
- □ **ground** 熟 fall to the ground 転ぶ
- □ **guard** 名①警戒, 見張り ②番人 動番をする, 監視する, 守る
- □ **guest** 名客, ゲスト
- □ **Guillaume Berlat** ギョーム＝ベルラ《人名》
- □ **guilt** 名罪, 有罪, 犯罪
- □ **guilty** 形有罪の, やましい
- □ **gun** 名銃, 大砲
- □ **gunshot** 名発砲

H

- □ **hall** 名公会堂, ホール, 大広間, 玄関
- □ **happen to** たまたま~する, 偶然~する
- □ **hardly** 副①ほとんど~でない, わずかに ②厳しく, かろうじて can hardly とても~できない

WORD LIST

- **hate** 動 嫌う, 憎む, (〜するのを) いやがる 名 憎しみ
- **have fun** 楽しむ
- **have got** 持っている
- **have nothing to do with** 〜と何の関係もない
- **hear of** 〜について聞く
- **heaven** 名 ①天国 ②天国のようなところ[状態], 楽園 ③空 ④《H-》神
- **helper** 名 助手, 助けになるもの
- **helpless** 形 無力の, 自分ではどうすることもできない
- **helplessly** 副 どうすることもできず
- **Henriette** 名 アンリエット《人名》
- **hid** 動 hide (隠れる) の過去, 過去分詞
- **hidden** 動 hide (隠れる) の過去分詞
- **hide** 動 隠れる, 隠す, 隠れて見えない, 秘密にする
- **hiding place** 隠れ場所
- **historic** 形 歴史上有名[重要]な, 歴史的な
- **hold up** ①維持する, 支える ②〜を持ち上げる ③(指を)立てる
- **Holmes, Sherlock** シャーロック゠ホームズ
- **honest** 形 ①正直な, 誠実な, 心からの ②公正な, 感心な
- **honestly** 副 正直に
- **honor** 動 尊敬する, 栄誉を与える
- **Horace Velmont** オラース゠ベルモン《人名》
- **horn** 名 警笛, ホーン
- **How could 〜?** 何だって〜なんてことがありえようか?
- **How dare you 〜!** よくも〜できるね。
- **however** 副 たとえ〜でも 接 けれども, だが
- **hung** 動 hang (かかる) の過去, 過去分詞

I

- **if** 熟 as if あたかも〜のように, まるで〜みたいに if only 〜でありさえすれば wonder if 〜ではないかと思う
- **imagine** 動 想像する, 心に思い描く
- **Imbert, Ludovic** リュドビック゠アンベール《人名》
- **Imbert, Madame** アンベール夫人
- **including** 前 〜を含めて, 込みで
- **indeed** 副 ①実際, 本当に ②《強意》まったく
- **inner** 形 ①内部の ②心の中の
- **innocence** 名 無罪, 潔白
- **innocent** 形 無実の
- **instant** 名 瞬間, 寸時 in an instant たちまち, ただちに
- **instead** 副 その代わりに
- **interested** 形 興味を持った, 関心のある
- **interesting** 形 おもしろい, 興味を起こさせる
- **iron** 名 鉄, 鉄製のもの 形 鉄の, 鉄製の
- **Italian** 形 イタリア(人・語)の 名 ①イタリア人 ②イタリア語
- **Italy** 名 イタリア《国名》
- **itself** 代 それ自体, それ自身

J

- **Jean Daspry** ジャン゠ダスプリ《人名》

The Adventures of Arsène Lupin, Gentleman-Thief

- **Jerland, Lady** ジャーランド夫人
- **jewel** 名 宝石, 貴重な人[物]
- **joke** 名 冗談, ジョーク
- **journey** 名 ①(遠い目的地への)旅 ②行程
- **joy** 名 喜び, 楽しみ
- **judge** 名 裁判官
- **jump out** 飛び出る
- **jump up** 素早く立ち上がる
- **just as** (ちょうど)であろうとおり
- **justice** 名 ①公平, 公正, 正当, 正義 ②司法, 裁判(官)

K

- **keep safe** 守護する
- **kindly** 副 親切に, 優しく
- **King Louis XVI** フランス国王ルイ16世
- **knife** 名 ナイフ, 小刀, 包丁, 短剣
- **knock** 動 ノックする, たたく, ぶつける 名 打つこと, 戸をたたくこと[音]
- **know** 熟 Who knows? 誰にわかるだろうか。誰にもわからない。
- **knowledge** 名 知識, 理解, 学問

L

- **L'Echo de France** エコー・ド・フランス《新聞名》
- **La Provence** プロバンス号《船名》
- **lack** 名 不足, 欠乏
- **Lacombe, Lous** ルイ=ラコンブ《人名》
- **Lady Jerland** ジャーランド夫人
- **last** 熟 at last ついに, とうとう
- **laughter** 名 笑い(声)
- **lay** 動 ①置く, 横たえる, 敷く ②整える ③卵を産む ④lie(横たわる)の過去 lay down 横たわる
- **le** 冠 《フランス語で英語のtheにあたる定冠詞で, 男性名詞の単数に付ける》
- **lead a life** 生活を送る, 暮らす
- **leave ~ alone** ~をそっとしておく
- **leave ~ for ...** …を~のために残しておく
- **leave in** ~をそのままにしておく
- **less** 形 ~より小さい[少ない] 副 ~より少なく, ~ほどでなく
- **lie** 動 ①うそをつく ②横たわる, 寝る ③(ある状態に)ある, 存在する lie down 横たわる 名 うそ, 詐欺
- **life** 熟 lead a life 生活を送る, 暮らす
- **lift** 動 持ち上げる, 上がる
- **light-colored** 形 明るい色の
- **list** 名 名簿, 目録, 一覧表
- **location** 名 位置, 場所
- **locksmith** 名 錠前師
- **long** 熟 for long 長い間 no longer もはや~でない[~しない]
- **look** 熟 look back at ~に視線を戻す, ~を振り返って見る look down at ~に目[視線]を落とす look for ~を探す look in 中を見る, 立ち寄る look out of (窓などから)外を見る look up 見上げる, 調べる
- **loudly** 副 大声で, 騒がしく
- **Louis Lacombe** ルイ=ラコンブ《人名》
- **Louis XIII table** ルイ13世様式のテーブル
- **Louis XVI, King** フランス国王ルイ16世
- **love** 熟 be in love with ~に恋して, ~に心を奪われて fall in love 恋におちる

Word List

- **lovely** 形 愛らしい, 美しい, すばらしい
- **lover** 名 ①愛人, 恋人 ②愛好者
- **lovingly** 副 かわいがって, 愛情を込めて
- **luckily** 副 運よく, 幸いにも
- **Ludovic Imbert** リュドビック＝アンベール《人名》
- **Lupin, Arsène** アルセーヌ＝ルパン
- **lying** 動 lie（横たわる）の現在分詞

M

- **madame** 名 ～夫人
- **Madame Andermatt** アンデルマット夫人
- **Madame Du Barry** デュ・バリー夫人
- **Madame Imbert** アンベール夫人
- **Madame Renaud** ルノー夫人
- **made of** 《be –》～でできて［作られて］いる
- **mademoiselle** 名 ～嬢
- **Mademoiselle Nelly Underdown** ネリー・アンダダウン嬢
- **main** 形 主な, 主要な
- **major** 名 少佐
- **Major Rawson** ロースン少佐
- **make sense** 意味をなす, よくわかる
- **Malaquis, the castle of** マラキ城
- **manner** 名 ①方法, やり方 ②態度, 様子 ③《-s》行儀, 作法, 生活様式
- **Marie-Antoinette** 名 マリー・アントワネット《フランス国王ルイ16世の王妃》
- **mark** 動 ①印［記号］をつける ②採点する ③目立たせる
- **marquis** 名 侯爵
- **Marquis de Raverdan** ラベルダン侯爵
- **Marquis de Rouzières** ルジェール侯爵
- **marriage** 名 結婚（生活・式）
- **marry** 動 結婚する
- **Massol, Officer** マッソル刑事
- **master** 名 主人, 雇い主, 師, 名匠
- **match** 動 ①～に匹敵する ②調和する, 釣り合う ③（～を…と）勝負させる
- **meaning** 名 意味, 趣旨
- **meeting** 名 集まり, ミーティング
- **mention** 動 （～について）述べる, 言及する
- **metal** 名 金属, 合金
- **middle** 名 中間, 最中
- **midnight** 名 夜の12時, 真夜中, 暗黒 形 真夜中の, 真っ暗な
- **might** 動 《mayの過去》①～かもしれない ②～してもよい, ～できる
- **mile** 名 ①マイル《長さの単位。1,609m》②《-s》かなりの距離
- **mind** 名 ①心, 精神, 考え ②知性 動 ①気にする, いやがる ②気をつける, 用心する
- **mix** 動 ①混ざる, 混ぜる ②（～を）一緒にする
- **modern** 形 現代［近代］の, 現代的な, 最近の
- **moment** 名 ①瞬間, ちょっとの間 ②（特定の）時, 時期 **at that moment** その時に, その瞬間に **for a moment** 少しの間 **one moment** ちょっとの間
- **Monceau, Parc** モンソー公園
- **monsieur** 名 ～氏《フランス語でMr./Sirにあたる敬称》
- **Monsieur and Madame d'Androl** アンドロル夫妻

- **most of all** とりわけ, 中でも
- **move away from** ～から遠ざかる
- **move to** ～に引っ越す
- **movement** 名 ①動き, 運動 ②《-s》行動 ③引っ越し ④変動
- **muddy** 形 泥だらけの, ぬかるみの
- **murder** 名 人殺し, 殺害, 殺人事件 動 殺す
- **murderer** 名 殺人犯
- **mystery** 名 ①神秘, 不可思議 ②推理小説, ミステリー

N

- **Nathan Cahorn, Baron** ナタン＝カオルン男爵
- **naval** 形 海軍の
- **navy** 名 海軍, 海軍力
- **nearby** 副 近くで, 間近で
- **necessary** 形 必要な, 必然の
- **necklace** 名 ネックレス, 首飾り
- **neither** 形 どちらの～も…でない neither ～ nor … ～も…もない 代 (2者のうち)どちらも～でない 副《否定文に続いて》～も…しない
- **Nelly Underdown, Mademoiselle** ネリー・アンダダウン嬢
- **nervous** 形 ①神経の ②神経質な, おどおどした
- **New York** ニューヨーク《米国の都市；州》
- **news** 名 報道, ニュース, 便り, 知らせ
- **newspaper** 名 新聞(紙)
- **next to** ～のとなりに, ～の次に
- **no doubt** きっと, たぶん
- **no longer** もはや～でない[～しない]
- **no one** 誰も[一人も]～ない no one else 他の誰一人として～しない
- **noble** 形 気高い, 高貴な, りっぱな, 高貴な
- **nobody** 代 誰も[1人も]～ない
- **noise** 名 騒音, 騒ぎ, 物音
- **none** 代 (～の)何も[誰も・少しも]…ない
- **nor** 接 ～もまたない neither ～ nor … ～も…もない
- **normal** 形 普通の, 平均の, 標準的な
- **not ～ at all** 少しも[全然]～ない
- **not ～ but …** ～ではなくて…
- **not quite** まったく～だというわけではない
- **not yet** まだ～してない
- **note** 名 ①メモ, 覚え書き ②注釈 ③注意, 注目 ④手形
- **nothing** 熟 have nothing to do with ～と何の関係もない
- **notice** 動 気づく
- **now** 熟 for now 今のところ, ひとまず from now on 今後 now that 今や～だから, ～からには
- **nowhere** 副 どこにも～ない

O

- **object** 名 ①物, 事物 ②目的物, 対象
- **occur** 動 (事が)起こる, 生じる, (考えなどが)浮かぶ
- **off to** 熟《be –》～へ出かける
- **offer** 動 申し出る, 申し込む, 提供する 名 提案, 提供
- **officer** 名 役人, 公務員, 警察官
- **Officer Delivet** ドリベ刑事
- **Officer Massol** マッソル刑事
- **one** 熟 this one これ, こちら one

WORD LIST

day (過去の)ある日, (未来の)いつか **one moment** ちょっとの間
- **oneself** 熟 **for oneself** 独力で, 自分のために **say to oneself** ひとり言を言う, 心に思う
- **Onfrey, Pierre** ピエール＝オンフレー《人名》
- **only** **if only** 〜でありさえすれば
- **onto** 前 〜の上へ[に]
- **open up** 広がる, 広げる, 開く, 開ける
- **opportunity** 名 好機, 適当な時期［状況］
- **ordinary** 形 ①普通の, 通常の ②並の, 平凡な
- **original** 形 独創的な
- **out of** ①〜から外へ, 〜から抜け出して ②〜から作り出して, 〜を材料として ③〜の範囲外に, 〜から離れて ④(ある数)の中から
- **Outard** ウータル《人名》
- **over** 熟 《be −》終わる
- **own** 熟 **of one's own** 自分自身の
- **owner** 名 持ち主, オーナー

P

- **P.S.** 略 追伸（= postscript）
- **painting** 名 絵（をかくこと）, 絵画, 油絵
- **Parc Monceau** モンソー公園
- **Paris** 名 パリ《フランスの首都》
- **passenger** 名 乗客, 旅客
- **patient** 形 我慢［忍耐］強い, 根気のある
- **pause** 動 休止する, 立ち止まる
- **pay** 動 支払う, 払う
- **pearl** 名 真珠
- **perfectly** 副 完全に, 申し分なく
- **perhaps** 副 たぶん, ことによると
- **photograph** 名 写真
- **pick up** 拾い上げる, 車で迎えに行く
- **Pierre Onfrey** ピエール＝オンフレー《人名》
- **pity** 名 哀れみ, 同情, 残念なこと
- **plain** 形 ①明白な, はっきりした ②簡素な ③平らな ④不細工な, 平凡な
- **play a part** 役目を果たす
- **play on words** 言葉遊び, しゃれ, 語呂合わせ
- **playing card** トランプ(の札)
- **pleasant** 形 ①(物事が)楽しい, 心地よい ②快活な, 愛想のよい
- **pleased** 形 喜んだ, 気に入った
- **pleasure** 名 喜び, 楽しみ, 満足, 娯楽
- **politely** 副 ていねいに, 上品に
- **possible** 形 ①可能な ②ありうる, 起こりうる
- **pour** 動 ①注ぐ, 浴びせる ②流れ出る, 流れ込む ③ざあざあ降る
- **powerful** 形 力強い, 実力のある, 影響力のある
- **prefer** 動 (〜のほうを)好む, (〜のほうが)よいと思う
- **press** 動 ①圧する, 押す, プレスする ②強要する, 迫る
- **pretend** 動 ①ふりをする, 装う ②あえて〜しようとする
- **priceless** 形 とても高価な, 金では買えない
- **pride** 名 誇り, 自慢, 自尊心
- **prison** 名 ①刑務所, 監獄 ②監禁
- **Prison de la Santé** ラ・サンテ刑務所
- **prisoner** 名 囚人, 捕虜
- **private** 形 ①私的な, 個人の ②民間の, 私立の ③内密の, 人里離れた

145

The Adventures of Arsène Lupin, Gentleman-Thief

- **probably** 副 たぶん, あるいは
- **professional** 形 専門の, プロの, 職業的な
- **proof** 名 証拠, 証明
- **proper** 形 適した, 適切な, 正しい
- **proud** 形 自慢の, 誇った, 自尊心のある
- **proudly** 副 誇らしげに
- **prove** 動 ①証明する ②(〜であることが)わかる, (〜と)なる
- **public** 名 一般の人々, 大衆
- **publish** 動 ①発表[公表]する ②出版[発行]する
- **pull out** 引き抜く, 引き出す, 取り出す
- **pull up** 引っ張り上げる
- **purpose** 熟 on purpose わざと, 故意に
- **push back** 押し返す, 押しのける
- **put ~ into ...** 〜を…に突っ込む
- **put back** (もとの場所に)戻す, 返す
- **put down** 下に置く, 下ろす
- **put in** 〜の中に入れる
- **put on** ①〜を身につける, 着る ②〜を…の上に置く

Q

- **Queen** 名 女王
- **quickly** 副 敏速に, 急いで
- **quietly** 副 ①静かに ②平穏に, 控えめに
- **quite** 熟 not quite まったく〜だというわけではない

R

- **Raoul** 名 ラウール《人名》
- **rather** ①むしろ, かえって ②かなり, いくぶん, やや ③それどころか逆に
- **Raverdan, Marquis de** ラベルダン侯爵
- **Rawson, Major** ローソン少佐
- **reach down** 手を下に伸ばす
- **reach over** 手を伸ばす
- **reach up** 背伸びをする
- **reality** 名 現実, 実在, 真実(性)
- **realize** 理解する, 実現する
- **recent** 形 最近の, 近代の
- **recently** 副 近ごろ, 最近
- **recognize** 動 認める, 認識[承認]する
- **record** 動 記録[登録]する
- **refuse** 動 拒絶する, 断る
- **regular** 形 ①規則的な, 秩序のある ②定期的な, 一定の, 習慣的
- **release** 動 解き放つ, 釈放する
- **Renaud, Madame** ルノー夫人
- **repeat** 動 繰り返す
- **reporter** 名 レポーター, 報告者, 記者
- **Republique** 名 レピュブリック広場
- **request** 名 願い, 要求(物), 需要
- **respect** 名 ①尊敬, 尊重 ②注意, 考慮
- **reveal** 動 明らかにする, 暴露する, もらす
- **revenge** 名 復讐
- **right away** すぐに
- **right now** 今すぐに, たった今
- **Rivolta** 名 リボルタ《人名》
- **rob** 動 奪う, 金品を盗む, 襲う
- **romantic** 形 ロマンチックな, 空想的な
- **rope** 名 網, なわ, ロープ

Word List

- **Rouen** 名 ルーアン《地名》
- **rough** 形 ①(手触りが)粗い ② 荒々しい、未加工の
- **Rouzières, Marquis de** ルジェール侯爵
- **Rozaine** 名 ロゼーヌ《人名》
- **Rubens** 名 (ピーテル・パウル・)ルーベンス《バロック時代のヨーロッパを代表する画家, 1577-1640》
- **Rue de Berry** ベリー通り
- **run away** 走り去る、逃げ出す
- **run into** ～に駆け込む、～の中に走って入る
- **rush** 動 突進する、せき立てる **rush into** ～に突入する、～に駆けつける、～に駆け込む **rush out of** 急いで～から出てくる

S

- **sadness** 名 悲しみ、悲哀
- **safe** 名 金庫 熟 **keep safe** 守護する
- **safely** 副 安全に、間違いなく
- **safety** 名 安全、無事、確実
- **sail** 動 帆走する、航海する、出航する
- **Saint Michel, Bridge** サン=ミシェル橋
- **Salvator** 名 サルバトール《人名》
- **sank** 動 sink (沈む)の過去
- **say to oneself** ひとり言を言う、心に思う
- **scared** 形 おびえた、びっくりした
- **scream** 動 叫ぶ、金切り声を出す
- **search** 動 捜し求める、調べる 名 捜査、探索、調査
- **secret** 形 ①秘密の、隠れた ②神秘の、不思議な 名 秘密、神秘
- **secretary** 名 秘書、書記
- **secure** 形 ①安全な ②しっかりした、保証された
- **see ～ as ...** ～を…と考える
- **seem** 動 (～に)見える、(～のように)思われる
- **Seine** 名 セーヌ川
- **sender** 名 送り主、荷主、発信人
- **sense** 名 ①感覚、感じ ②(-s)意識、正気、本性 ③常識、分別、センス ④意味 **make sense** 意味をなす、よくわかる
- **sentence** 名 文
- **separate** 形 分かれた、別れた、別々の
- **serious** 形 ①まじめな、真剣な ②重大な、深刻な、(病気などが)重い
- **servant** 名 ①召使、使用人、しもべ ②公務員、(公共事業の)従業員
- **set free** (人を)解放する、釈放される、自由の身になる
- **shake** 動 ①振る、揺れる、揺さぶる、震える ②動揺させる
- **shape** 名 ①形、姿、型 ②状態、調子 **in the shape of** ～の形をした
- **sharp** 形 ①鋭い、とがった ②刺すような、鋭い ③鋭敏な ④急な
- **shelf** 名 棚
- **Sherlock Holmes** シャーロック=ホームズ
- **shocked** 形 ショックを受ける
- **shone** 動 shine (光る)の過去、過去分詞
- **shook** 動 shake (振る)の過去
- **should have done** ～すべきだった(のにしなかった)
- **shut** 動 ①閉まる、閉める、閉じる ②たたむ ③閉じ込める ④shutの過去、過去分詞 **shut in** ～に閉じ込める
- **sick** 熟 **feel sick** 気分が悪い
- **side** 名 側、横、そば、斜面
- **silence** 名 沈黙、無言、静寂 動 沈

147

黙させる, 静める

- [ ] **silent** 形 ①無言の, 黙っている ②静かな, 音を立てない ③活動しない
- [ ] **silently** 副 静かに, 黙って
- [ ] **similar** 形 同じような, 類似した, 相似の
- [ ] **simply** 副 ①簡単に ②単に, ただ ③まったく, 完全に
- [ ] **sit up** 起き上がる, 上半身を起こす
- [ ] **situation** 名 ①場所, 位置 ②状況, 境遇, 立場
- [ ] **skill** 名 ①技能, 技術 ②上手, 熟練
- [ ] **skilled** 形 熟練した, 腕のいい, 熟練を要する
- [ ] **slid** 動 slide (滑る) の過去, 過去分詞
- [ ] **slip** 動 滑る, 滑らせる, 滑って転ぶ
- [ ] **slowly** 副 遅く, ゆっくり
- [ ] **snore** 動 いびきをかく
- [ ] **so** 熟 and so そこで, それだから, それで so ~ that … 非常に~なので… so far 今までのところ, これまでは so that ~するために, それで, ~できるように
- [ ] **so-called** 形 いわゆる
- [ ] **society** 名 社会, 世間
- [ ] **softly** 副 柔らかに, 優しく, そっと
- [ ] **solution** 名 ①分解, 溶解 ②解決, 解明, 回答
- [ ] **solve** 動 解く, 解決する
- [ ] **someday** 副 いつか, そのうち
- [ ] **somehow** 副 ①どうにかこうにか, ともかく, 何とかして ②どういうわけか
- [ ] **someone** 代 ある人, 誰か
- [ ] **something** 代 ①ある物, 何か ②いくぶん, 多少
- [ ] **somewhere** 副 ①どこかへ[に] ②いつか, およそ
- [ ] **sorry** 熟 be sorry for doing ~して申し訳なく思う feel sorry for ~をかわいそうに思う
- [ ] **source** 名 源, 原因, もと
- [ ] **steal** 動 ①盗む ②こっそりと手に入れる, こっそりと~する
- [ ] **stole** 動 steal (盗む) の過去
- [ ] **stolen** 動 steal (盗む) の過去分詞
- [ ] **stone** 名 ①石, 小石 ②宝石
- [ ] **storm** 名 嵐, 暴風雨
- [ ] **strangely** 副 奇妙に, 変に, 不思議なことに, 不慣れに
- [ ] **stranger** 名 ①見知らぬ人, 他人 ②不案内[不慣れ]な人
- [ ] **struck** 動 strike (打つ) の過去, 過去分詞
- [ ] **struggle** 動 もがく, 奮闘する
- [ ] **style** 名 やり方, 流儀, 様式, スタイル
- [ ] **submarine** 名 潜水艦
- [ ] **succeed** 動 ①成功する ②(~の) 跡を継ぐ
- [ ] **success** 名 成功, 幸運, 上首尾
- [ ] **successfully** 副 首尾よく, うまく
- [ ] **such a** そのような
- [ ] **sudden** 形 突然の, 急な
- [ ] **suggest** 動 ①提案する ②示唆する
- [ ] **support** 動 ①支える, 支持する ②養う, 援助する
- [ ] **suppose** 動 ①仮定する, 推測する ②《be -d to ~》~することになっている, ~するものである
- [ ] **surprised** 形 驚いた
- [ ] **surprising** 形 驚くべき, 意外な
- [ ] **surround** 動 囲む, 包囲する
- [ ] **suspect** 動 疑う, (~ではないかと) 思う 名 容疑者, 注意人物
- [ ] **swindler** 名 詐欺師
- [ ] **sword** 名 ①剣, 刀 ②武力

Word List

T

- **take** 熟 take ~ to … ~を…に連れて行く take a walk 散歩をする take back ①取り戻す ②(言葉, 約束を)取り消す, 撤回する take from ~から引く, 選ぶ take off (衣服を)脱ぐ, 取り去る, ~を取り除く, 離陸する, 出発する take out 取り出す, 取り外す take out of ~から出す
- **talk of** ~のことを話す
- **telegraph** 名 電報, 電信
- **that** 熟 so ~ that … 非常に~なので… so that ~するために, それで, ~できるように
- **theft** 名 盗み, 窃盗, 泥棒
- **theory** 名 理論, 学説
- **there is no way** ~する見込みはない
- **therefore** 副 したがって, それゆえ, その結果
- **Thibermesnil, the castle of** ティベルメニル城
- **thief** 名 泥棒, 強盗
- **thin** 形 薄い, 細い, やせた, まばらな
- **think of** ~のことを考える, ~を思いつく, 考え出す
- **this one** これ, こちら
- **though** 接 ①~にもかかわらず, ~だが ②たとえ~でも 副 しかし
- **thoughtful** 形 思慮深い, 考え込んだ
- **threaten** 動 脅かす, おびやかす, 脅迫する
- **throw out** 放り出す
- **thrown** 動 throw (投げる) の過去分詞
- **tie up** ひもで縛る, 縛り上げる, つなぐ, 拘束する
- **time** 熟 at one time ある時には, かつては at that time その時 at the time そのころ, 当時は each time ~するたびに
- **tired** 形 ①疲れた, くたびれた ②あきた, うんざりした
- **tool** 名 道具, 用具, 工具
- **torn** 動 tear (裂く) の過去分詞
- **transom** 名 ドアや窓の上に取り付けた, ちょうつがいで開けられるようになっている小さな長方形の窓
- **traveler** 名 旅行者
- **treasure** 名 財宝, 貴重品, 宝物
- **treat** 動 扱う
- **trial** 名 裁判
- **trick** 名 ①策略 ②いたずら, 冗談 ③手品, 錯覚
- **trouble** 熟 get into trouble 面倒を起こす, 困った事になる, トラブルに巻き込まれる
- **true to** 忠実に
- **truly** 副 本当に, 真に
- **trust** 動 信用 [信頼] する, 委託する
- **truth** 名 ①真理, 事実, 本当 ②誠実, 忠実さ
- **tunnel** 名 トンネル
- **turn around** 振り向く, 向きを変える, 方向転換する
- **turn away** 向こうへ行く, 追い払う, (顔を) そむける, 横を向く
- **turn in** 向きを変える
- **turn on** ①~の方を向く ②(スイッチなどを) ひねってつける, 出す

U

- **unable** 形 《be – to ~》~することができない
- **unchanged** 形 変化していない
- **undress** 動 衣服を脱がせる, 着物を脱ぐ
- **unkind** 形 不親切な, 意地の悪い
- **unless** 接 もし~でなければ, ~し

The Adventures of Arsène Lupin, Gentleman-Thief

なければ

- **unsigned** 形 署名されていない
- **untie** 動 ほどく, 解放する
- **upstairs** 副 2階へ[に], 階上へ
- **used** 動 ①use (使う) の過去, 過去分詞 ②《- to》よく〜したものだ, 以前は〜であった 形 ①慣れている, 《get [become] - to》〜に慣れてくる ②使われた, 中古の

V

- **vacation** 熟 on vacation 休暇で
- **Valorbe** 名 バロルブ《人名》
- **Varin, Alfred** アルフレッド=バラン《人名》
- **Varin, Etienne** エティエンヌ=バラン《人名》
- **Velmont, Horace** オラース=ベルモン《人名》
- **very well** 結構, よろしい
- **victor** 名 勝者, 優勝者
- **Victor Danègre** ビクトール=ダネーグル《人名》
- **victory** 名 勝利, 優勝
- **visitor** 名 訪問客

W

- **wagon** 名 荷馬車, ワゴン (車)
- **wait for** 〜を待つ
- **wake up** 起きる, 目を覚ます
- **walk** 熟 walk across 歩いて渡る, walk along (前へ) 歩く, 〜に沿って歩く walk around 歩き回る, ぶらぶら歩く walk away 立ち去る, 遠ざかる walk out of 〜から出る walk up to 〜に歩み寄る
- **wallet** 名 札入れ
- **warfare** 名 戦争, 交戦状態, 戦闘行為

- **warmly** 副 温かく, 親切に
- **warn** 動 警告する, 用心させる
- **Watteau** 名 (アントワーヌ・) ヴァトー《フランスの画家, 1684–1721》
- **way** 熟 in a way ある意味では in any way 決して, 多少なりとも there is no way 〜する見込みはない way of 〜する方法 way to 〜する方法
- **wealthy** 形 裕福な, 金持ちの
- **well** 熟 very well 結構, よろしい
- **well -ed** 《be -》よく [十分に] 〜された
- **what ... for** どんな目的で
- **What about 〜?** 〜についてあなたはどう思いますか。〜はどうですか。
- **whatever** 代 ①《関係代名詞》〜するものは何でも ②どんなこと [もの] が〜とも 形 ①どんな〜でも ②《否定文・疑問文で》少しの〜も, 何らかの
- **while** 熟 after a while しばらくして for a while しばらくの間, 少しの間
- **Who knows?** 誰にわかるだろうか。誰にもわからない。
- **whom** 代 ①誰を[に] ②《関係代名詞》〜するところの人, そしてその人を
- **Why not?** どうしてだめなのですか。いいですとも。ぜひそうしよう!
- **will** 熟 free will 自由意志
- **willing** 形 ①喜んで〜する, 〜しても構わない, いとわない ②自分から進んで行う
- **wine** 名 ワイン, ぶどう酒
- **wireless** 形 無線の
- **woken** 動 wake (目が覚める) の過去分詞
- **wonder** 動 ①不思議に思う, (〜

に）驚く ②（～かしらと）思う **wonder if** ～ではないかと思う 名 驚き（の念），不思議なもの
- **wooden** 形 木製の，木でできた
- **word** 熟 **play on words** 言葉遊び，しゃれ，語呂合わせ
- **work in** ～の分野で働く，～に入り込む
- **work of** ～の仕事
- **work of art** 芸術品
- **worried** 形 心配そうな，不安げな
- **worse** 形 いっそう悪い，より劣った，よりひどい
- **worst** 形 《the –》最も悪い，いちばんひどい
- **worthy** 形 価値のある，立派な
- **wound** 名 傷
- **write back** 返事を書く
- **writing** 名 ①書くこと，作文，著述 ②書き物，書かれたもの，文書 **in writing** 書面で

Y

- **yet** 熟 **and yet** それなのに，それにもかかわらず **not yet** まだ～してない

E-CAT

English Conversational Ability Test
国際英語会話能力検定

● E-CATとは…
英語が話せるようになるためのテストです。インターネットベースで、30分であなたの発話力をチェックします。

www.ecatexam.com

iTEP

● iTEP®とは…
世界各国の企業、政府機関、アメリカの大学300校以上が、英語能力判定テストとして採用。オンラインによる90分のテストで文法、リーディング、リスニング、ライティング、スピーキングの5技能をスコア化。iTEP®は、留学、就職、海外赴任などに必要な、世界に通用する英語力を総合的に評価する画期的なテストです。

www.itepexamjapan.com

ラダーシリーズ
The Adventures of Arsène Lupin, Gentleman-Thief
怪盗ルパン傑作短編集

2011年11月3日　第1刷発行
2023年12月2日　第6刷発行

原著者　モーリス・ルブラン

リライト　寺沢美紀

発行者　浦　晋亮

発行所　IBCパブリッシング株式会社
〒162-0804　東京都新宿区中里町29番3号
菱秀神楽坂ビル
Tel. 03-3513-4511　Fax. 03-3513-4512
www.ibcpub.co.jp

© IBC Publishing, Inc. 2011

印刷　株式会社シナノパブリッシングプレス
装丁　伊藤理恵　　カバー・本文イラスト　菊地玲奈
組版データ　Sabon Roman + Didot Bold

落丁本・乱丁本は、小社宛にお送りください。送料小社負担にてお取り替えいたします。本書の無断複写(コピー)は著作権法上での例外を除き禁じられています。

Printed in Japan
ISBN978-4-7946-0106-3